Ulf Löwenhav

The Power *of* Active Thinking

How to Become a Resilient Contrarian Through the Strength of Engaged Thinking

Published by
LID Publishing Limited
The Record Hall, Studio 204,
16-16a Baldwins Gardens,
London EC1N 7RJ, UK

info@lidpublishing.com
www.lidpublishing.com

A member of:
BPR
Business Publishers Roundtable

www.businesspublishersroundtable.com

Printed in Latvia by Jelgavas Tipogrāfij
ISBN: 978-1-912555-36-9

Cover and page design: Matthew Renaudin

Ulf Löwenhav

The Power *of* Active Thinking

How to Become a Resilient Contrarian Through the Strength of Engaged Thinking

LID

MADRID | MEXICO CITY | LONDON
NEW YORK | BUENOS AIRES
BOGOTA | SHANGHAI | NEW DELHI

Contents

1

Introduction

This book is about change or, more to the point, how you can improve your decisions by detecting and managing your own inherent weaknesses.

During 2017, I enrolled in a new research project on boardroom performance at Henley Business School, where I investigated how important financial corporate decisions are processed. The background to my interest was that I for years had seen truly dysfunctional processes and decisions among all levels of corporate decision-makers, people we would assume were truly professional. The process would start with management's preparations in the boardroom and finally presenting proposals to the shareholders. Focusing on a seemingly minor decision in this way was very revealing. First, the narrow focus enabled me to see the limited financial understanding on all the layers of an organization. I could see that for the study of a corporate environment, insights into psychology and sociology would become extremely useful, more so than knowledge of traditional business subjects. Second, it revealed that many decisions were poor, populistic and not founded in real business understanding. I think there has been a general assumption that established organizations are run in a professional way, which I had gradually realised is outright false. So, I wrote this book to enable students and decision-makers in corporations and organizations to see how weak and useless our decision making can be and how it can be possible to become more useful through the understanding of our environment.

This book addresses the practical implications of behavioural economics for real decision makers – corporate managers and directors. It is based on my research at Henley Business School as well as on my experience of lecturing on behavioural governance at the Stockholm Business School. In these lectures, I used seminal work by Daniel Kahneman and Yuval Harari, in particular *Thinking, Fast and Slow* by Kahneman, which although a bit heavy reading for most students, can change people profoundly. *Sapiens: A Brief History of Humankind* by Harari also has the ability to make people revaluate their role in a bigger system. These texts, which give profound insights into our weaknesses and how to manage them, make people more reflective, humble and, I think, turn people into better decision-makers. My research shows that at times, managers base their decisions on theories they haven't really understood, instead of considering who their key stakeholders are. For instance, many managers get their first introduction to finance in MBA programmes, without understanding the basic accounting and principles behind the key area of financial decisions.

Through my experience, I have discovered that many decision makers are looking for new inputs on decision making and for practical clues about how to get started. They have read new texts from the growing area of behavioural economics and feel they are gradually building a better understanding of their own shortcomings and biases, but they still need to see how to deal with their own situations – and how to turn theory into a better daily behaviour.

Psychologists are aware that our brains are in different states of activity. Sometimes we are extremely relaxed. This is where we are most of the time and this has been called system 1. Sometimes we are actively engaged, which is system 2. Kahneman refers to system 1 as passive thinking, and system 2 as active thinking. What Kahneman calls system 1 – characterized by our lack of true awareness and fast, passive, and often poor, decisions – is a major problem for managers and key decision makers. System 2 – the ability to pull oneself together, take a step back, and confidently enter into a room of active and more logical thinking is hard work. Being a contrarian in such situations and bringing something new to the discussions is often met with concerted resistance, and most people are uncomfortable with the social stigma it often results in.

Although we may understand system 1 – thinking intuitively – the application of it into management decision making is seldom done. Often, we like to think that we are aware and conscious thinkers without the necessary effort.

This book also addresses anthropological areas, in particular the concepts of myths and the power they convey; and neo-tribalism as a powerful explanation of our fears and general behaviour. My research shows that we are deeply affected by the tribes we live in and aspire to be part of. My belief is that tribalism is alive and kicking in organizations and once we see this invisible force, we may become better decision makers.

I have also entered into the realms of philosophy with regards to power structures and group self-control.

This text ends with the use of Kahneman's insights into decision making to exemplify an alternative route to analyse the context of a major decision.

Finally, the purpose of this book is to allow you to become a more active thinker, to force yourself into system 2, to steer the corporate ship in line with the corporate purpose and be a useful asset to your company. In order to succeed, you need to get your bearings and be resilient. In short, you need to be a contrarian, and a sternly resilient one.

2

The Power *of* Passive Decision Making: System 1

"A reliable way of making people believe in falsehoods is frequent repetition, because familiarity is not easily distinguished from truth."

Daniel Kahneman

Imagine a situation where you are wrong about something that you have taken for granted. Well, this happens every day. Let me give you a universally understandable example.

Every day at the Louvre Museum, people spend hours queuing up to view the *Mona Lisa* painting. The truth is that the painting became well known after it was stolen from the Louvre by an Italian gentleman, Vincenzo Peruggia, in 1911. The painting was known in the art world as it was painted by Leonardo da Vinci, but Vincenzo managed to take the painting under his coat and walk out from the Louvre. Some two years after the theft, when Vincenzo was trying to make money on the painting, he was arrested, and the painting was sent back to Paris. Following this, several articles were published about patriotism and whether art by the Italian da Vinci should be in Italy, and so the painting with its warped smile became famous. So, the hordes of people lining up at the Louvre are passive thinkers. They misunderstand why the painting is famous and take it for granted that it is a masterpiece. An active thinker would gauge the art and make up their own mind.

Do we want to be part of that queue or should we make our own decisions?

The single largest challenge for a decision maker is to really think, therefore, to think actively. It is like the difference between sitting in the front seat of a car – behind the steering wheel – and sitting in the back seat. Sitting behind the wheel you control the car and actively guide the vehicle forward. In the back seat you may think you are part of the driving process, but the truth is that you can only watch what happens. For those who have read Daniel Kahneman's *Thinking, Fast and Slow*, this comes as no surprise, but simply knowing this difference doesn't make the challenge smaller or easier. Similarly, you can read and understand a book, but to see the real change you need to change your behaviour.

There is power in knowing about your system 1 and system 2 and how your brain works. Kahneman estimates that the brain power associated with system 1 passive thinking, or tacit knowledge, is 220,000 times more powerful than our system 2 active thinking. System 1 is where we are most of the time. When we really put effort into solving a difficult issue, we become smarter, we enter system 2 and navigate consciously among facts to try to make logical decisions. We may notice the difference when, for example, walking and talking on our mobile phones at the same time. This works fine until we face more difficult situations. For example, when we move from a simple 2+2 calculation – where we effortlessly find with the right answer – to, say, a more complicated calculation, like 348 x 45. In more difficult situations, we subconsciously slow down and stop to enable our limited system 2 thinking to do the calculation. This is when we become logical and process our thoughts in a conscious manner.

Another example is when a golfer can see the difference in their thinking when they putt for par. At first, they are relaxed and often not very focused – system 1. If they, however, miss that putt and face the embarrassment of a bogey and maybe even a double bogey, they feel the pressure and concentrate really hard, going from system 1 into the powerful system 2, to get all of their focus into the important putt.

In a similar way, we can go from system 2 into system 1. A simple example is when we learn to ride a bicycle. At first, we struggle with the difficult coordination of moving the pedal and keeping the balance. After a while, it becomes tacit knowledge, and we move our processing from the burdensome and slow system 2 into the fast and easy system 1.

In order to fully grasp the difference between systems 1 and 2 it is helpful to consider the example of sitting in the front seat of a car or in the back seat with somebody else driving mentioned earlier. With system 1, where we are almost all the time, we sit in the back seat and solutions are handed to us. In this way, when making decisions we don't actively navigate facts to arrive at clever decisions; our decisions are spontaneous reactions. For example, we put on our jacket when we are cold, or eat when we smell food and become hungry. This process is performed by our system 1 with its amazing power, and it is difficult to comprehend that our solutions are not clever and conscious. We would rarely acknowledge the fact that we are not in control. Focusing is hard work, so we have system 1 to help us survive without being constantly active.

The concept of passive thinking is challenging for most people. While we are willing to agree that other people are poor decision makers, it is difficult for us to believe that we are not logical and present thinkers. But, as we will see, we are in system 1, because it is fast and allows us to survive. In fact, the major decisions we make, such as finding a partner, are scarcely a product of logical selection. Ask yourself or somebody close to you which logical facts led them to end up with a particular person. I think in most cases we have no idea; we just feel an attraction. It may be small, or we are attracted to looks and certain attributes. On the other hand, if our partner selection used the system 2 process, we would think more about factors like financial security or reliability, but we rarely get this far. We have already been led by our subconscious to a final and prepared decision.

In a similar way, we may be handed a fully prepared decision, complete with rational arguments to back it up. For instance, when our favourite sports team plays a game, we often fail to see fouls and mistakes of 'our' players and only see those of the opposing team. This behaviour has been documented in carefully monitored experiments where people watched the same game but were randomly told to support a particular team. The result showed that the people noticed that 'their' team made fewer mistakes and that it was the opposing team that played rough. This is neo-tribalism at its finest: when whatever we see just supports our view and when we fail to see things that go against us. Kahneman calls this confirmation bias, and it can be seen at play when a close friend is quarrelling with their partner and we quickly support our friend and deem them faultless. This may be fine, but only if we are aware of it.

In a similar fashion, we fail to see the shortcomings of our own friends and relatives when they are in arguments with other people and quickly choose their sides. Again, this is because we are in the back seat and are handed decisions. This wouldn't necessarily be a problem if we had more awareness of our own shortcomings.

Part of our system 1 thinking is our search for tribes and glorious belonging. Soccer is a great example of this. We see how soccer clubs invoke strong feelings in their supporters who follow the matches and feel a strong need to show their connection to 'their' club. If supporters have a successful day, they share in the success of their team and feel fulfilled. The need to feel fulfilled is also true for supporters who have a successful day as they need a constant reminder of success. This is key for system 1 to work beneficially and is reinforced when we feel fulfilled through success.

Our system 1 and system 2 thinking modes are crucial in the financial world, where availability of capital and interest rates are constantly fluctuating. Such fluctuations lead to varying levels of demand, so at times the value of our properties increase and, as our borrowing is mostly fixed, we see how our net asset value rises. When we analyze these changes using our system 2 thought process, we can see how increased wealth is not the product of being clever, but rather a consequence of economics. But this is where there is a danger if our system 1 thought process kicks in and makes us believe that we are clever, leading to rash decisions. It may lead us to feel overconfident in our ability to make more money and sell our house to buy a more expensive one. This may be a fine decision to make until the interest rates turn against us, or the banks, which also have collateral cycles, make property investment more difficult. In the beginning of a financial bubble, we usually see the price increase of properties but play it cautiously. Later, as we gradually become confident, we are blinded by how easy it was to become rich and consider price increases to be normal and expected.

Our minds are programmed to perform in this way because we are short-term rather than long-term survivors. By seeing and accepting our mental shortcomings, we can build systems to detect what is going on and jump from the back seat to the front. We could create rules for decision making processes and live better, less risky and more secure lives.

We experience short-term survival in our working environments too, where influential managers through their chosen agenda or their body language compromise our options. If we are not fully aware or trained to see what is happening, we are 'handed' a decision and thoroughly feel that it is a good one. This is because when in the system 1 thought process (short-term survival mode) our mind goes through the various alternatives and hands us the best and safest option in only a few split seconds. If the manager's agenda is beneficial to us, we don't search for potential additions, but just accept what is handed to us. The problem is that in the cases when we unconsciously feel that they may not tolerate opposition, we may, in the name of survival, unconsciously choose to be agreeable, to agree to be in the back seat. When this happens, we have little or no awareness of our shortcomings.

Can we refuse to accept the decisions that are being handed to us? Yes, we can. We have an ongoing surveillance of our own decision making which prevents us from making decisions that may be bad for us. But the problem is – as we shall see during the next few chapters – we are quite useless at scrutinizing the various powers around us and poor at scrutinizing our own decisions.

In the past, our ancestors lived in caves and were exposed to the natural elements. Natural selection during the last few thousand generations has promoted fast, passive thinking in us and has led to the development of our current behavioural mechanisms. When coming across a snake, the majority of individuals would use their system 1 thought process and jump away to survive. Whereas individuals who are able to utilize their system 2 thought process may pick up the snake to study it. This is a very basic look at natural selection, but essentially the individuals who would have used their system 2 thought process were less likely to survive.

So, are our natural abilities suited for key decision making posts in organizations? Not really. At least eight areas of the working environment demonstrate how our inherent behavioural abilities stand in the way of making good decisions:

1. Social skills
2. Recruitment
3. Trends
4. Forecasts
5. Symmetry
6. Seduction
7. Sustainability
8. Low awareness

Social skills

In the past, we needed to have social skills to survive as hunters/farmers. Similarly, today we need to cooperate with others, which means creating relationships and fitting in. This often requires being friendly and helpful; however, these social skills are not what make a great manager or director. We all want to be liked – consciously or unconsciously – and facing the risk of not been seen as a competent manager affects our behaviour. Therefore, we often choose the easy, safe and popular option. We avoid taking the risk to initiate new and radical processes, because although it may be better for the company, we are more worried about people not liking it. In addition, there are many people who never see the problems, or have new initiatives and participate in the decision making only in the way that is "good" for them; in the back seat.

Recruitment

The instinct for survival makes us evaluate people based on evident attributes like friendly behaviour or a smiley face. When we meet someone, we scrutinize their face, and, for example, look for a smile in the hope of eliminating danger. While we cannot truly evaluate people's attitudes or abilities from their faces, we still do it. This behaviour transcends into the workplace when new management is being recruited. Our inherent nature leads us to find people who are just like ourselves. Such situations can be problematic because our weak ability to step away from the decision making process means that we are likely to rank friendly clones as the best candidates for the job, regardless of how professionally competent they really are.

Trends

A crucial part of being a corporate director or manager is the strategic thinking involved in navigating the corporation through threats or opportunities. This requires the ability to study the business environment and understand what is happening. In the forest, we are able to hear the slightest crack of a branch or see the smallest leaf moving – we are constantly monitoring risks to our survival. However, our ability to spot changes in the corporate landscape is very limited. Although a lot of information is now available through the internet, we still fail to see new competitors, changing customer behaviours or a new development in our business climate.

It has been said that if you place a frog in a pot of water that slowly increases in warmth, it will not notice the rising temperature and so will eventually be boiled. In a similar way, we are not equipped to see gradually changing conditions. Managers suffer this fate too, falsely believing that others will be able to see the ongoing changes until it's too late.

Forecasts

A central part of organizational success is driven by the ability to predict the future business environment and its potential for growth. This may sound like a rational exercise but often we are too presumptuous and unrealistically positive, which results in predictions that are not based on reality and forecasts that are so off that they are of no use. This is particularly striking when looking at the development of start-ups that overwhelmingly fail.

Forecast-related decisions are not limited to revenue and costs structure and are also related to interest rates and access to loan facilities. These are matters heavily influenced by politics and banking regulations, matters that we have no insights into. However, it appears that we continue to tell ourselves to trust our forecasting abilities without doing an analysis – it is almost as if we believe that it would be wrong to not make a forecast. This bad and powerful behaviour makes us produce useless forecasts. It's an example of passive back seat thinking.

In an experiment to explore this, we asked MBA students to consider two imaginary and completely different investment funds. The first was the 'Skilled' fund, which was roughly the historic performance of Madoff's funds, one of the largest financial frauds ever. The second was the USEQ1 fund, which just showed substantial volatility.

When we asked the MBA students which fund they would invest in, some 90% chose the steady 'Skilled' fund. This is because in general people don't like volatility and want their money to grow securely, in a predictable way, so that we can estimate our wealth. To the MBA students, the USEQ1 fund appeared shaky and raised the risk that they might lose some of their investment on it. Scary stuff. See graph below:

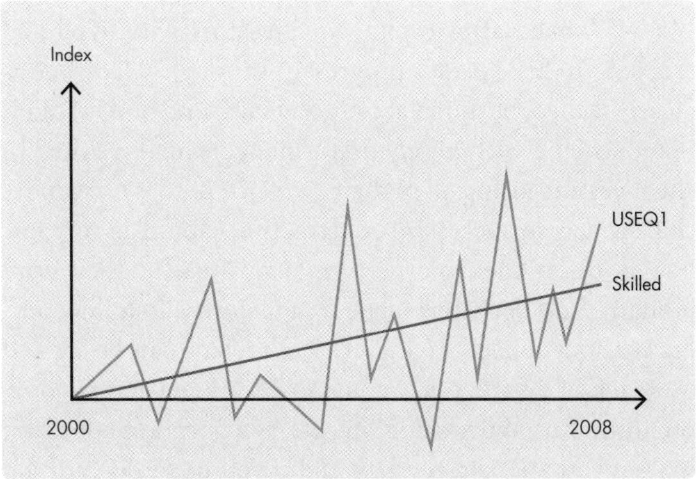

Source: Ulf Löwenhav, Stockholm Business School (September 2018)

We all know that equity markets are volatile and, irrespective of the talents of a fund manager, it is necessary to hold on to investments long enough as they go through various cycles. So why do people seek to invest in something so unrealistic? Such risks could be eliminated, if we jump-started our system 2 and thought logically. Instead, most people in such situations use system 1, the decision is handed to them and so they go for an easy solution. In many ways this is what happened to Bernard Madoff, founder of Bernard L. Madoff Investment Securities. Madoff looked after capital for investors who liked and trusted in his steady 'progress'. Although Madoff was clearly skilled, he didn't act in good faith and built a fraudulent scheme with phony performance which resulted in the investors losing all of their money. There is no wonder that he was so successful at attracting capital as very few people questioned his performance; instead they were jubilant. The decisions made by a majority, to follow others without reflection and critical review, can be viewed as a lack of awareness; we just don't know what is going on around us and we don't react. As a corporate decision maker, you are paid to react and if you don't do your job you are basically useless.

Symmetry

We have a weakness for symmetrical shapes. For example, we consider symmetrical faces to be more beautiful, and we like a company better if it has steady growth rather than turbulent performance. Just like in the Madoff situation above, what we think is good and safe does not necessarily correspond to reality.

When comparing our desires that are still here from our hunting days, it is easy to understand why we appear to resist change; it is not symmetrical, it is something new and it deviates from the past. However, as a corporate decision maker, having the tendency to resist change can be a serious flaw. How can we navigate our corporations through turbulence with new competitors striking from the right, changing consumer patterns hitting us from the left and digitalization in the back, if we don't want to make decisions that change the 'symmetry'? We can't, so it is important to try to understand ourselves why we are reluctant to make a decision that brings about change and try to pinpoint what makes a decision uncomfortable. If it is just change that is holding us back, maybe we should go ahead and make the decision.

Seduction

Our belief that we are rational can be seen in how we organize our sales efforts. We assume that we should display the actual advantages of our products, such as price or functionality. It is a backward system 1 assumption that our customers are system 2 buyers. In reality, if we analyze the situation, we can understand that we need to be in system 2 to see what is going on and that our customers are in system 1, i.e. that they are not rational and purchase decisions are served to them by their emotions and impulses. When we accept that our customers are in system 1 and are passive thinkers, we realize that the best way to sell to them is to communicate with their emotions. So, if we want to be successful, we need to view the sales process as a seduction, getting clients to like us and our products rather than to see their advantages.

Sustainability

In the business world we are in many ways heading towards some type of collision, meaning one party will be hurt. Consequently, business sustainability is about being a contrarian and finding the best way to prevent threats by changing direction. Being a contrarian doesn't only mean that you try to view issues from a different perspective; it should also involve sharpening your skills so that you become aware of changes that take place slowly and are not always noticeable. This can include gradually increasing debts or issues that ought to be addressed, but are often not on a formal agenda.

Many businesses claim that they are becoming more sustainable, but still pursue short-term over long-term interests. There are many issues that can catch a business by surprise – and so have a black swan effect. There are many examples of these, including the destruction of our planet, widening pay gaps and the frequencies of financial crises. The first (assumed) financial crisis took place in the 1600s as a result of speculation in the price of tulip flowers. The following financial crisis took around 100 years to develop. Since the depression of the 1930s, we have seen an increase in the frequency of financial crises and the typical perspective before a new crisis starts is that "this time is different". This is a true human weakness as we have a low ability to analyze trends, in particular if we are part of one ourselves. When the economy is strong, we like it so much that we are not able to see or take the pain of a new depression and so we turn a blind eye to the signs.

Low awareness

There are many cases where corporate decision makers were in the system 1 mode of thinking and might have performed better if they understood their low level of awareness. An interesting case is that of the Swedish telephone and mobile network operator, Telia Company. In 2007, with a mission to expand, Telia made the decision to enter Uzbekistan. However, without taking the right precautions the company ended up making a large investment in one of the world's most corrupt countries, where the move was investigated for possible bribery accusations. Three former Telia executives were acquitted by a Stockholm court in February 2019. But with a higher level of awareness and the courage to explore and speak up about this move, Telia managers could have been more involved in setting the investment parameters – this was no ordinary market expansion – this was a beach full of mines.

Readers of *Sapiens* by Yuval Noah Harari and *Thinking, Fast and Slow* by Daniel Kahneman will recognize that we are passive thinkers (system 1) and very dependent on continuous social acceptance. Our understanding of the world, order, purpose and relationships can be used in a comprehensible way. And ongoing comprehensible narrative where we base our existence in the story of our past and future direction are helpful and have a strong connection to the rules surrounding our norms and how we behave. It would be impossible to quickly and continuously make the decisions required in the working environment if we didn't accept that at least some passive thinking occurs in individuals. Active thinking (system 2) can be too burdensome, except for sporadic hard thinking. However, it is possible to develop our ability to think critically.

Managers on all levels require the ability and guts to review, analyze and resist what is being said and the agenda-setting of colleagues. They need the ability to ignore factors like traditions, cues and references to how others are making decisions. The challenge is to continuously refer back to the true purpose of the organization and the interests of stakeholders whilst being strong enough to admit your own lack of knowledge. For instance, with financial decisions we may trust others with making decisions to avoid showing our lack of understanding of the subject.

The above-mentioned factors are key to understanding our behaviour. However, there is one more issue we need to address to complete our perspective. Our fear of losing something, our loss aversion, is of fundamental importance. According to psychologists, the fear of loss is a stronger drive than our interest in potential gain. The strong urge to avoid risk is coded in our brains. Loss aversion has a major influence on our decision making and makes us less rational. For instance, we avoid snakes without having first-hand experience of their potential danger. And as those of our ancestors that avoided snakes lived to have us as offspring, we carry the loss aversion gene.

Those who picked up a snake for more careful analysis were more likely to have died. Avoiding risks is in our genes and we encounter this every day. In the professional environment, this is evidenced by our preference for staying on the proven and safe path for fear of losing our positions, saying things that we think others will agree with and avoiding financial and strategic risks.

Insights into system 1 and system 2 can be used to guide our professional lives. In this environment, it is very useful to understand the behaviour of fellow managers. Are your fellow management colleagues' decisions a result of loss aversion – agreeing with the chairman or other board members and considering the risk of deviating from the common understanding – or the fruit of a conscious system 2 analysis? Are we just following traditions or the paths of peer companies, or do we in the interest of serving our stakeholders, have the guts to take a contrarian route, to be the first to deviate towards conscious decision making?

Being in system 1 and making decisions that are fast and easy is what most people do every day. It is difficult to change, and unfortunately most people don't even know how to change or even how to start to have a conscious desire to change. However, by having a better understanding of the decision making process we can enable more reflection and logical analysis. And we can see and understand that almost everything around us is the product of man-made theoretical constructions. All theories, rules and orders have been created by someone, somewhere, at some point; so, welcome to the next chapter about myths.

3

The Power *of* Myths

"Academics lack perspective. In a debate on whether the world is round, they would argue, 'No', because it's an oblate spheroid. They suffer from 'the curse of knowledge': the inability to imagine what it's like not to know something that they know."

Steven Pinker

Myths are associated with urban legends and false stories, but they are more than that. They reveal fundamental human concepts and are crucial for our understanding of the world. The reason I have included academic theories as myths is that they are not only man-made creations. People in general think academic theories must be right because academics should know how things work. As a result, we often think that academic theories fully answer various problems, while they are often simplified concepts of a complex reality.

In *Sapiens*, Harari addressed the concept of order, how we understand the world, how it was created, what our purpose is and where we are going. Maybe we need myths to make the complex nature of the world into something more understandable. This is similar to how and why we construct a narrative. While a narrative is an individual way of seeing how we fit in in the world and giving us direction, myths are stories created by individuals or society at large to help us make sense of the world collectively.

Myths are man-made, but we believe them. In this way, myths are different from fables which we may believe in as kids, but which we learn and understand are not real as we grow older. The table on the next page shows the relationship between how we make sense of the world and different types of stories, organized by claim (x-axis) and how truthful they are (y-axis). For example, we don't know for certain whether or not legends are true – some may be while others are too incredible to be believed.

Similarly, history is an exact retelling of what happened on a particular occasion in the past, but its claim to absolute credibility can be questioned based on the sources. In terms of power, myths are stronger than fables, legends and history. Myths benefit from having authoritative explanations of how things work and may provide us with a simplified concept. Depending on your views, you may perceive religion to be a paradigm myth – a man-made construct. In another perspective, scholars see religion as made of orders created to give people meaning, order and to keep them working.

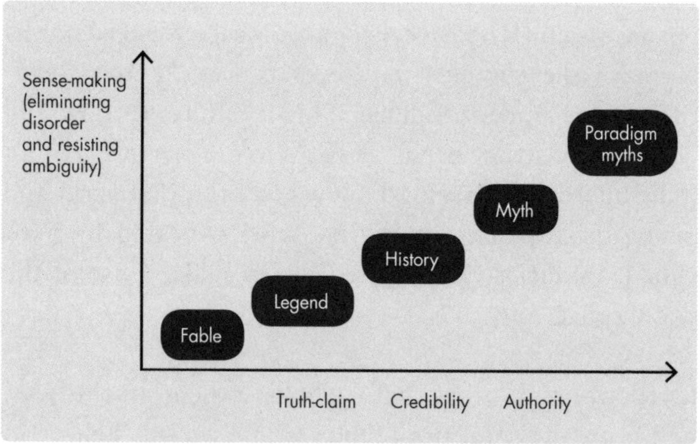

The Myth-truing Logic Proposition

The causal relationship between narratives and sense-making.

Source: Bruce Lincoln

When Donald Trump claims that the major newspapers engage in fake news, his claim has some merit. Everything we think and have opinions about and that we take for granted is built on an order of things. In this instance, many major newspapers are perceived to be guardians of established perspectives and the status quo. Furthermore, we expect and assume that journalists don't have an agenda in their analysis and reporting, that they just gather and decipher information. This is quite naïve. Journalists too are carriers of myths and each brings their own perspectives and biases to their writing. Fake news may not always be fake, but it is certainly skewed. This can be changed with time by creating increased awareness around reporting and its inherent bias. Back to Trump, by being totally contrarian with regard to established publishers and news sources, he continues to stir controversy, invites reflection and critical thinking, and may in fact lead journalists to the path of unbiased reporting.

The entire dogma of financial theory can be viewed as a series of strong myths. They have flaws, but the cornerstone theories themselves have few alternatives. The main established financial theories are rooted in the challenge that physicists saw in the incomprehensible behaviour of traded stocks. These early researchers were not interested in finance, accounting or even the stock market but were told by investors about the irrational behaviour of stock prices. They were convinced that just as with natural science, there had to be correlations to be discovered. These early pursuits led to theories of market equilibrium and efficiency which subsequently paved the way to portfolio theory. During this evolution, there were also emerging perspectives of shareholder focus. Milton Friedman was a professor at University of Chicago in the 1960s and 1970s and a pioneer for the concept that the duty of management was to focus on the enrichment of shareholders. After Friedman, the focus shifted to include other stakeholders, and today there are leading theorists that consider the management team to be the main beneficiary of enterprise success.

The quantitative focus of financial theories separates them from the other management sciences. One reason for this is that finance and accounting academics think that they are dealing with very precise tools and that the qualitative research and knowledge in the social sciences are vague. In fact, there is the view that a strategy professor and a finance professor at the same university are so far apart that they cannot even communicate. The strategy professor may see the need for disruptive material changes in strategy, but the finance professor will use empirical data to claim a massive risk premium and kill the discussion and the entire project. While finance scholars usually have a total acceptance of the complex theories of finance, the majority of people find finance and the workings of capital markets totally incomprehensible. Finance professionals claim that this black box of finance is correct and until new and better theories arrive, the quants have the power to claim that they are right.

A cornerstone of modern finance is the capital asset pricing model, or CAPM. This is a descriptive model of the relationship between risk and return. The positive relationship between risk and return implies that the more risk there is, the more return investors require. So, if a company can estimate the risks, then it can calculate the return investors need, which will indirectly affect the share price. The resulting profit and estimated risk will produce a value of the company and therefore a share price. This is a great and useful descriptive base that has become a normative model which managers will use to maximize the share price. If the risk can be measured precisely, with the forecast profit as given, then surely an increased dividend and more borrowing will increase the return and thereby the share price! It is just that the relationships between factors affecting share price are more dynamic and complex than those suggested by the model. Correlation does not imply causality. However, the strength of this approach is that it is something to build on. And there are no alternatives on the horizon.

The model was gradually developed by several great academics at various North American universities of which University of Chicago has taken the lead. The US has also fostered the concept of business and management education, and finance theories from the base of various MBA programs. Most people have no concept of equity markets and finance when they start an MBA program, and their first introduction is likely to include the CAPM, which describes the relationship between risk and expected return for an asset. Initially, students may find it difficult, but gradually they will develop an understanding of risk and return and its convenience when dealing with financial decisions.

In a similar way, finding a perfect balance of debt and equity capital is the key to making the right investments and making financial decisions. Approaching anything finance-related with CAPM becomes a habit, like cycling or smoking. Once you are familiar with the process, you find it easily approachable, but it may be that it is not necessarily right. Like religion, financial theories become paradigm myths. If someone has alternative thoughts, then that person is viewed as a heretic. Financial concepts have become a habit and similarly to the way in which a myth becomes part of society's structure of belief, the habit is very hard to change. All current finance academics have grown up with CAPM, and for many, the word finance is synonymous with CAPM and its view of risk. So, the student that studies organizational behaviour in relation to a financial decision will be puzzled. Investors don't behave like they are supposed to according to CAPM and the major cluster of theories surrounding the financial decision. To start with, a logical assumption is that an organization should retain its earnings if it has good investment prospects – better than the prospects of its shareholders. This shareholder opportunity cost is an understandable and logical assumption. It becomes slightly more difficult when trying to exclude the investments that do not reach the target – the cost of the capital being used. The Miller-Modigliani theorem states that leverage doesn't matter much as the increased cost of loans with increased leverage is offset by less dependence on expensive equity. So, leverage should not matter under perfect conditions and it should not matter for the shareholder if his or her funds are in the firm or paid out in the form of dividends. Except that investors seem to care a lot. And these investors appear to not trust management's use of retained funds. The result has been a theory without any support in CAPM, referred to as bird-in-hand theory, implying that investors want to see all excess cash in the firm paid out to shareholders. So, directors and managers appear to look at the bird-in-hand demands of investors and take a short-term populist position. In such situations, what is the value of the directors or top management? Are they not there to make decisions?

So, we end up with dominant theories, accepted widely, but built on assumptions referred to as garbage by Eugene Fama, Nobel laureate and considered the father of modern finance. But they are still untouchable. System 1 dominates the decisions of organizations, since directors and managers with financial studies backgrounds see CAPM as fundamental to investment and dividend discussions. Furthermore, cementing the relationship between financial myths and management behaviour is the force of interconnecting directorships. When management relies on traditional finance theories, it can be incredibly difficult to argue against such established views.

Stepping away from such myths is easier said than done. It is not only a logical challenge, but a social one too.

People will refer to theories, peer-companies, traditions and other system 1 arguments. A contrarian is the person that goes against such common views and traditions and adopts their own perspective. Warren Buffett is considered to be one of the best investors alive. Buffett doesn't follow daily finance articles like everybody else, because he knows that it is not profitable to be a follower. He dares to buy unpopular stocks and sell popular ones. Directors or managers should do the same. They are paid to navigate the company in a logical way and not according to turnkey thoughts. However, the contrarian decision maker, the one that is extremely useful to stakeholders and dares to perform in a logical way, is less likely to be re-elected and less likely to have friends among his fellow decision makers. People don't like contrarians, and people don't like people leaving the safe cluster of myths.

Anchoring is when someone establishes a position to which everything else will be related. In negotiations, this is when somebody presents a low bid and establishes a level around which negotiations will develop. Myths have the potential to establish frames and it becomes difficult to totally disregard the anchors that are subsequently developed. In finance, we find it very difficult to even discuss alternative views of anchored finance terms connected to the myths we may want to change. No matter what you think, you need to create change using the same terms as your potential opponents, irrespective of their incorrectness.

4

A Behavioural Take *on* Financial Theories

Following on from the previous chapter, which deals with myths, it would be worthwhile to point out some differences you end up with when you take a contrarian view on financial theories. The list may not be exhaustive as we are likely to gradually add new perspectives and alternative views on finance.

The following is a brief collection of alternative takes on financial theories:

1. Decisions
2. Stakeholders
3. Debt
4. Cost of capital
5. Dividend
6. Risk
7. Market efficiency
8. Advisors
9. Profit and cash flow
10. Financial branding and reputation
11. Fractional ownership
12. Tension
13. Price/earnings ratio
14. Calculus
15. Valuations

Decisions

Decision making is not a quantitative science. People like to think that we are thinking machines with some emotions, but we are more like emotions-in-motion with some computing skills. The concept of rationality is focused on our ability to reason and solve problems by analysis. This makes sense and we would like to be part of the tribe of rational thinkers. But decision making is far too complex a process for us to know what is going on, or for us to be in control of it. Really, it is the powerful processes in the brain that make decisions all the time and make sure we are happy with them.

In the case of financial decision making, it would be great if it was this simple. Finance experts would argue that while to a large extent we are controlled by our emotions, when it comes to major decisions that have financial implications, we are rational and make decisions that will maximize our net worth.

However, this is not always the case. Let us start by looking at the process of buying a house. It is a big decision, so we make a list of the important things that we require, prudent things like proximity to a bus station and an efficient heating system. It may also be that we require an extra bedroom that we can use as a guest room and home office. But, when we come to the lovely little house, we just can't resist it. The minute the real estate agent asks us how we would decorate it; the powerful endowment effect kicks in and we can see ourselves living there. Suddenly, we own this house with an old, inefficient heating system and with no easy access to public transport. We also have no room for our friends when they visit. What happened is that the powerful relationship of our emotions made the decision for us. But now we have to explain to our friends and family what happened. This is the only time when we are rational: to find explanations and excuses. We construct a narrative to justify why the house was the right decision.

With financial decisions in particular, it is evident that short-term thinking controls our long-term survival, and, to that end, we have to make laws preventing potential reckless behaviour. This is the case with pensions savings. Without the mandatory saving schemes forcing us to set aside money for our pensions, few people would keep in mind this financial consideration; they would all use up their money in the short term, be left with nothing on retirement and be a big burden to society.

There are many more examples of how the short term controls our behaviour including smoking, getting tattoos, having just one more glass of wine before driving and eating too much of the wrong things. The list is long. The key insight is that we do not stand a chance against our emotions and our egos.

Our choices are based on our preferences. We buy cars and we get married because of our preferences, and we don't feel the need to find rational explanations as to why we have the preferences that we have. That is just what we like. In the same way, with our financial decisions we may choose to invest in companies because we like them, or their management, or their products, or because we just like the name.

Applying this understanding to the CAPM relationship between risk and return, we see that we assign risk to investments. There are various ways that investment risk can be measured with various financial returns, depending on how keen the investor is to buy the particular share. However, the purchase decision is a causal effect of liking, not simply risk and return.

The CAPM assumes that we think in terms of risk and return, and that risk increases gradually. In reality, we are more likely to look at investments as being binary: either there is no risk or there is a risk. And if there is risk, we may avoid making the investment altogether. However, maybe risk is not part of the equation. Maybe we categorize an investment based on how strategically well-placed it is for us or our organization, or perhaps simply on whether we like the investment. This could explain some market valuations. In the graph on the next page, we see some companies organized according to how strategically well-positioned they are, and how well-liked. A company like H&M has a strong strategic position and is well-liked, placing the company strongly in terms of unconscious investment behaviour and therefore contributing to a high value. Other companies, such as Atlas Copco, are superbly well placed strategically, but people don't have any emotions for the brand. Banks are generally in awkward strategic positions and not liked. Atlas Copco is unlikely to receive a superior market value through just making more money and growing more; they also need to be seen and be admired by customers and investors. IKEA is not a listed company but if they were, their customers would like to be shareholders and they would be valuable. Apple is another example of a company that is in an excellent strategic position and well-liked. The company has a devout following not only among its customers but also its employees.

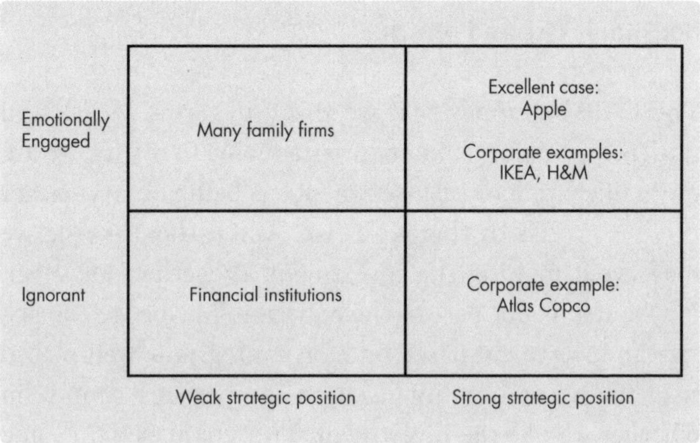

The Emotion

Strategic position matrix.

Stakeholders

After Milton Friedman, we have become used to the idea that shareholders are the premier stakeholder group. However, a successful company should involve all stakeholders who want to continue to contribute. Sometimes, as long as there is some profit, the management team are left to continue to run the company and protect their remuneration packages. While shareholders do have legal power over the company, they need to attend annual general meetings to have the opportunity to voice their views to other shareholders, management and the board. However, increasingly, shareholders don't see their holdings as long-term, so they don't become involved in trying to change the company.

When I was growing up, it was common that one inherited shares from one's parents and sat on them for some 20 or 30 years. A few years ago, the common holding time for a share was a few years and now it is down to some nine months. This practice of short-term holding is common among both private individuals and institutional shareholders. As a result, management can continue to influence the selection of directors and auditors. Legally, the board is elected by the shareholders, but if they don't get involved, then management controls the process. This also applies for selecting auditors, which should be an independent process. In reality, it is important that management gets along well with the auditors and should they want to change auditors, shareholders go along with no questions asked.

Debt

Taking on borrowed funds has become so common that nobody questions it. In fact, finance courses teach us that there is an ideal mix of equity and debt that can optimize the cost of capital. Having debt is seen as natural and continues to be a basic assumption when one builds a business.

However, there are many people that, given their experiences and their subsequent loss aversion, don't want any debt. So, a little debt is not just a little more risk, it is an inconceivable option. And this may be where finance professionals differ from ordinary people. In finance, debt is natural; for many others, it is not. This means that the established theories regarding cost of capital may not be very relevant. Indebtedness among private individuals and non-financial organizations has increased steadily over the last few years, most likely as a function of quantitative easing and low interest rates. Investment bankers and advisors tell business owners and management that they should increase dividends and borrow to make acquisitions. Why? Because the assumption is that debt is cheaper than equity and, in many cases, financial professionals know exactly how much cheaper it is based on the study of thousands of corporations.

Today, we are living with a fragile economy where there are many interconnecting relationships between banks in terms of interdependence of borrowings and various forms of swaps. But as there are often unexpected events, sometimes referred to as black swans, it is difficult to understand if management allows debt to increase simply because their competitors have done so, or because they have learnt from the results of financial theories while toying with the life-savings of pensioners and widows that are vested in the company.

There is so much capital going around that taking on debt should not be an automatic assumption, but a strategic decision: some companies unnecessarily transfer volatility into share prices, making the stock unattractive. The reason for investing in a particular equity is to get the upside of that company or that industry. Instead, in many cases, it has become a play on interest rates. It would be more ethical for investors to find their own leverage by borrowing against their portfolio.

Debt is a system 1 assumption and in many cases the assumption may be correct. But, because the risk of bankruptcy is directly linked to debt, debt should not be an automatic choice. In summary, debt may be the biggest ongoing and often unnecessary threat to business, and it should be a system 2 choice.

Cost of capital

Based on a collection of dominant financial theories, we can determine the cost of the capital used. Essentially the idea is that high volatility means a high cost of equity. This is done by looking at the assumed cost of equity and the true cost of debt. CAPM plays a role here, along with studying how a company's share price fluctuates in relation to other stocks. This is a beautiful theory but it assumes that we are rational when dealing with financial returns.

As a psychologist, I would prefer to look at the attachment investors have to particular investments. Some companies (or investments) are well liked, which means that irrespective of their financial performance or volatility, there are people who want to own shares – they are not driven by potential financial returns like dividends or increasing share prices. The result is that the company's cost for issuing shares can be seen as being cheaper, and, putting it in financial terms, the cost of equity becomes less than the cost of debt.

Many companies rank investment opportunities and compare them against the cost of capital, the assumption being that if the return on investment is higher than the cost of capital, the investment should be made. But this simplification assumes that we know the opportunity cost.

It may well be that we optimize our return on equity by paying high dividends, minimizing our equity portion. But if owners have no better use for the received dividends than to keep them in the bank, maybe we should think again. Maybe we should retain their money in the firm and use it to make a few more investments.

Management and directors should try to estimate the cost of capital, and at the same time complement the use of established theories by asking shareholders and other stakeholders about their preferred debt level and alternative uses of funds as the key input for the dividend decision process.

Dividend

The overriding key to understanding the dividend decisions is that they are underestimated while being crucial strategic decisions. Managements that just replicate the dividend policy of competitor organizations or go with the populist route recommended by investment bankers are not doing enough. This can be attributed to the poor quality fruit of system 1 thinking. Management has the responsibility to search for a balanced dividend policy.

The key assumption is to decide whether cash flow generated by the firm should stay in the company and be reinvested or be paid out to shareholders. The criteria to follow is where the funds will benefit the company and its stakeholders. This means that the decision-makers - the management - need to consider all investment alternatives, the risk and expected return, and compare this with the opportunities this gives their shareholders.

Following the core principal idea, the Miller-Modigliani theorem implies that shareholder wealth is not affected by the dividend; if the funds are transferred to their wallet or stay in the firm, their accumulated wealth is constant. This means that markets should not care about an organization's dividend policy and shareholders should be grateful for the absence of a dividend; the share price should in fact go up, as this means that management has lined up some great investment opportunities. However, markets and investors don't behave like they are supposed to. It appears as if markets go up when organizations report higher dividends, which goes against the grain of the theory; why own a part of a company if all you want is to pull your funds out?

The answer to this is that investors don't trust management. With the increasing strength of the role of management, shareholders fear that funds will be invested in a way which may be good for the management, but not necessarily good for the shareholders. This fear boils down to fundamental governance issues.

A closer look at dividend policies suggests that organizations establish such policies based on populist findings. The value of dividends agreed for distribution to shareholders by an organization often has no relationship to the core of investing – funds should be used in the company if it has superior investment alternatives to that of its shareholders. The populist route to decision making is not wise and management should consider changing business conditions and the banking climate.

The carelessness of investors and management alike is striking. To mistrust management means that you are not there for the long term. It is also a poor sign to have management that is more invested in securing re-election at the AGM than to manage the firm in a way that maximizes the present value.

As the dividend decision has far-reaching consequences for solvency and liquidity, managers or directors need to work to maximize present value. This means that everybody involved needs to increase their awareness and make logical decisions. This means making a conscious decision to consider the perspectives of the organization and its stakeholders and understand the best interests of both. Relying on financial theory is a good start, but more in-depth thought is required.

Risk

The expectation that decision-makers are rational is part of the problem, along with low awareness and low levels of responsibility. This is a function of short-terminism among other things. We are well-adapted to survival in nature – we can see the movement of a leaf – and we live outside wild nature, including living in the current flow of information. Unlike movements in nature, we have no tools to see trends or movements in our corporate landscape. Our low levels of awareness are bad for those involved in risk management. This is further accentuated by our reliance on system 1 thinking, where we adapt populist measures and follow peer companies and advisors without making up our own mind.

The opposite graph shows how corporate non-financial debt in selected countries has constantly increased faster than their gross domestic product (GDP). The reason appears to be that there are more funds available enabling inexpensive borrowing, thereby increasing the risk of bankruptcy. Our low awareness and cognitive weaknesses are not part of the established financial theories. So, what is the likelihood of your average manager knowing that the organization's debt has been increasing gradually during the last ten years? It is low, and they are likely to say that it hasn't increased more than that of other organizations. This is exactly the problem;

we don't know what is going on and don't appear to want to know.

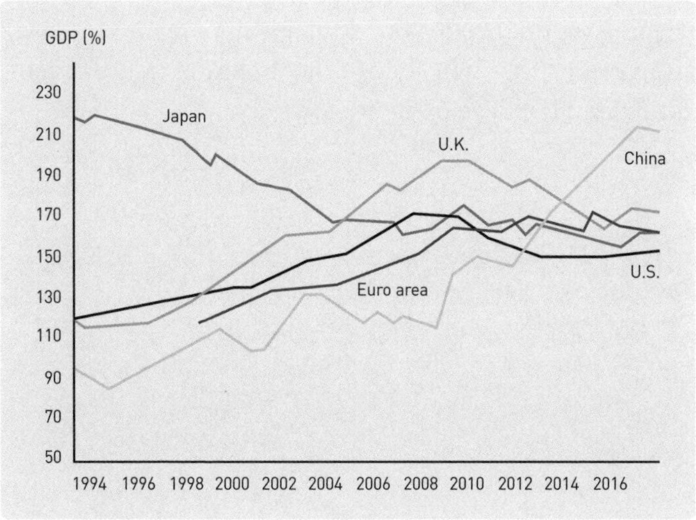

Corporate non-financial debt as percentage of GDP, for selected countries and Euro area

Source: BIS (March 2018)

The black swan concept refers to the fact that we may never have seen a black swan and the probability is low that we will ever see one. But in fact, they do exist. Similarly, when we say that a dramatic interest-rate increase has a low probability, this doesn't mean that it isn't possible. And if this unlikely but still possible event (a 'black swan event') occurs, things may go really wrong. So, it is not the job of management to gamble on the likelihood of interest-rate changes, as they are taking huge risks with other people's money. Management needs to know what is going on financially and strategically prepare for black swan events that will change the direction of the organization and the development of society.

Market efficiency

Given how the human mind works, with all its cognitive weaknesses, it is difficult to see how the market would be perfect. The 19th and early 20th century French physicist turned economist, Léon Walras, focused his attention away from equilibriums in nature to equity markets in order to explain chaotic equity prices. His assumption was that all markets are constantly searching for an equilibrium, so equity prices should come to a rest. Then, when something changes, equity prices will be in search of a new resting point, just like a ball in a bowl. Walras was originally a physicist and believed there was a straightforward explanation for everything. Capital markets could be understood and therefore forecasted.

The founding father of modern macro-economics, John Maynard Keynes, reviewed capital markets but realized that they were far too complex to understand. He concluded that the understanding and forecasting of human decisions was impossible as everybody has different backgrounds and different preferences. Keynes likened this to a beauty contest where in order to forecast who will win, we have to understand the preferences of the individual judges. If this sounds like a difficult undertaking, then equity markets would be even more challenging as there we are dealing with millions of equities and billions of potential investors. Keynes' insights into capital markets are probably right but because we are dealing with so much data, and in particular money, we rely on established and nice theories to forecast decision making. While these theories are useful to some extent, they are not reliable because they are simplifications of something far more complex.

What we have is a man-made construct about how markets are built and operate – a myth. The entire dogma of financial theories, headed by numerous Nobel prize laureates, is a paradigm myth, too comprehensive and too widely accepted as eternal truth to change – just as with religions. As with religious belief, which individuals can follow without understanding in full, we have created simplifications that allow people to have faith in a financial structure.

It is striking that decision makers in capital markets, be they analysts or investment managers, have so much faith in the theories that they have studied at school and believe that the markets are both efficient and possible to forecast. Even the press continues to follow quarterly reports of companies as if they were useful indicators of future performance. Instinctively I think we all know that the theories don't work well. But, as everybody else appears to believe in the theories, we continue to accept them as well. We would hate to admit that they might not be right or that their underlying assumptions do not correspond to reality.

Advisors

In financial theories, decisions and markets work well without the influence of bystanders, the people that gather around the financial streams of large corporations. The most influential bystanders may be investment bankers who influence decision makers; they have connections and insights into the actions of competitors. However, their most important task may be to boost the confidence of CEOs, management and senior directors so as to provide a platform on which major strategic decisions are made.

The connection to the markets is a key service. There is no doubt that the investment banks have direct access to the workings of the market, but they also create a risk for conflicts of interest and short-term behaviour. The relationship with influential investment bankers creates a strategic advantage or a potential disadvantage, so not having the contact and allowing for these strong influences may not be an option.

The networks of investment bankers and of management consultants can be seen as an invisible web of global political and financial influence. Their relatively strong connection to capital markets enables bankers to claim to have superior knowledge on how to read markets, even if this isn't necessarily true. Many corporate decision makers feel they need to maintain strong ties with management consultants and, when possible, engage the firms, maintaining a strong flow of information. This allows bankers and consultants to help strengthen and maintain current financial myths.

With a growing need to appear more transparent in business, journalists who report on the daily financial status of organizations have become powerful. Daily business reporting is built around the assumption of market equilibrium and that every financial change has an impact. Although this may be completely wrong at times, just because journalists print it readers assume it to be correct, and the management are forced to follow the tune of short-termism.

Profit and cash flow

The concept of profit comes from the way we account for our business dealings and how we have to report our finances. The profit shown in our accounts determines our income taxes and our room for dividends, but this is where its usefulness ends. The key information we look for is the firm's ability to generate cash flow. Profit has to some extent become a poor proxy for cash flow. People generally know this but continue to focus on profit rather than cash flow.

Financial branding and reputation

Branding has a strong connection to system 1, as it guides fast decision making. Using fame, feeling and fluency, or the 3Fs, it is possible to see how decisions can be made.

a. Fame means that we recognize something, and if we have had some contact with a brand previously, we recognize it fast. Just as when we enter a grocery store and recognize the colours of Coca-Cola, the same is true for certain organizations in the equity markets. Regardless of whether the fame is good or bad, it is just that we see it and relate to it. It is important to see that there are hundreds of thousands of listed companies and that it would be impossible to evaluate them one by one. So, we see the ones that are famous and often ignore the rest. These never get to the evaluation phase.

b. Feeling comes next and relates to immediate responses. The process is unconscious, and we are passengers in the back seat, where the driver is our intuition. All actions affect us. For instance, a bank that doesn't treat its customers well may see their share price decline. But this also means that a brand with positive feeling like Apple could use its brand in a different way, such as banking. Since Apple has the technology and customers that like them, they would be a formidable competitor in the banking markets, maybe in particular among younger people who are not traditional about their banking choice.

c. Fluency is the distinctiveness of the brand – if the brand can make people choose it and make a purchase, or if the brand can make people decide to turn positive feelings into action.

The entire concept of financial branding goes against the grain of general financial theory with its quantitative focus – that we as investors are driven by risk and return. The study of financial markets uses the term perception to deal with discount rates for valuation purposes. But, unlike fast moving consumer markets where branding is everything, perception is deemed to have a fractional effect in capital markets, simply because of the assumption that investors are very rational.

Reputation is the shadow of branding, and large organizations spend vast sums on analysing and maintaining the reputation of the organization, the board and that of the chairman and the CEO. Companies could learn a lot from continuous tracking of their reputation and their brand. It is quite easy to track a firm's valuation in relation to competitors over time and study the correlation to qualitative issues like reputation. It is revealing to see changes in valuation over time, with the introduction of new management or through acquisition processes and dividend announcements.

The study of reputation can be very revealing if done indirectly. Indirect questions can tell us more about the reputation of an organization because we may still answer what is expected of us if posed a direct question. We can get a perspective on an organization's reputation if we ask analysts both direct and indirect questions. For example, the Swedish technology and engineering company Sandvik has a strong institutional recognition. But when students were asked to what extent they wanted to work for the organization it became clear that many, in particular women, saw little future there. In this case, Sandvik is famous, but appears to have little feeling. If people don't want to work there, they certainly are not going to buy shares or perhaps even their products. This weak employer reputation cannot be isolated, because the reputational component is often carried over into all kinds of markets.

Fractional ownership

To a large extent the success of capitalism comes from the transfer of the founder's own liability to that of the company, and the owner's liability becomes limited to the amount invested. The other crucial contributing factor is that of fractional ownership, whereby you can own parts of shares of a company. This enables easy fundraising as investors could manage their liquidity and spread the ownership in an easy way. However, clever entrepreneurs maintain control of their company and clever investors own enough so that they have de facto control. While they may not necessarily have absolute control, they have enough to be the largest shareholder when all the owners meet at the annual general meeting.

It is important to review exactly what control shareholders have. If a shareholder holds the majority (more than 50% of the votes), alone or together with a strategic partner, this enables the shareholder to appoint all the directors of the company; not just some, but all. The shareholder that controls the management can continue to run the business largely for their own benefit, appointing themselves or family members to other important positions. As long as the business is run within legal limits, there is nothing the other shareholders can do. They may in fact be left outside the economic benefits of the firm altogether as the majority shareholders can prevent the dividend payout.

Shares are traded and are expected to be worth the fraction of the wealth that they represent. So, when we hear earnings announcements that send the value of the firm higher, the value of the fractional ownership should be unchanged due to no control over future payouts.

Tension

Tension is pressure. We behave differently as pressure increases and our decisions become increasingly altered. Tension is a major component in all decision making and can be used to your advantage.

We see decision makers as 'somewhat emotional' analysts while they are actually 'somewhat analytical' emotionalists. This carries all the way through into the management team. When people come under pressure and become uncomfortable, they need to let off steam and want to leave the discomfort of system 2 and fall into the comfort of system 1. They might fool themselves into believing that they are in control, but they have become passive thinkers, leaving the exposed front seat in preference for the cushier back seat. The result of this is not trivial – the best time to sell or buy a company from someone is when the individual involved is under tension. We have seen the price of a company double or lose most of its value when individuals go through the emotional swings that may happen because someone places them there, or because of self-infliction. In any case, this may be exactly the time to act. The mood of financial decision makers is not included in the financial theories, but it can be important and should not be ignored.

Price/earnings ratio

The price/earnings ratio (P/E ratio) is the ratio of an organization's share price to its earnings per share. The 'P' in the above ratio is the market price while the 'E' is the profit after tax. We frequently read articles about equity markets based on the assumption that stocks with a low P/E ratio are cheap, while the ones with a higher level are more expensive. There are many hidden problems here and the key thing is that we are not rational. We do not base our decisions on future projections only. More importantly, we have to have a positive sentiment in order to buy stock, so when comparing, say, two banks, we will find that one bank would have a lower P/E value than the other based on their assumed future income and capital, the difference in fact being that we just prefer ownership in one more than in the other. So, stocks may continue with a low P/E ratio for some time while not necessarily being cheap. The other point to consider is that profit itself is not a good indicator of performance as profit is heavily adjusted for factors such as tax.

Calculus

A basic assumption in financial theory is that investors base their decisions on some form of financial and quantitative logic. This is not so in reality. Just one piece of evidence may be the reverse split phenomenon, whereby two or more shares are merged. If you combine two shares, it would be reasonable to assume that the share price would double. However, this is seldom the case. As investors 'feel' – and as their system 1 delivers the idea – the price has increased: it is time to sell! The result is a negative effect on the share prices. People may be able to calculate, but the fact that system 1 is so powerful makes this ability a bit useless.

Valuations

Traditionally, when a project or discussion requires valuations, the assumption almost always focuses on net asset value or using discounted cash flow (DCF). When using net asset value, the asset is priced using assumptions such as estimated future cash flows. This is because it is a dominant assumption, or myth, in finance. However, a problem is that we are not very quantitative and are driven by emotions. As a result, we end up making decisions not based on quantitative calculations, but more based on what we feel and want. So, the discounted cash flow method is in reality used to check decisions already made and to make sure that the valuations are roughly right. Financial theories are also useful when all parties have a finance background, as it provides all parties in a negotiation with a language and a tool that can enable a transaction. The consequence is that valuations are completely different things than prices. Market value is what the investor will pay based on emotions and biases and the theoretical value is what we use in trying to find a rationale for the price paid. This creates a great division between professionals that would like to see us people as rational, quantitative investors driven by financial facts and a more qualitative perspective, driven by students of psychology and behavioural economics. Because of the numerical exactness of financial theories, they are not easily challenged and, as a result, financial analysts often hang on to the main financial theories, although they know that they are very often quite useless.

Financial theories are a language

The main function of the established financial theories, such as discounted cash flows or the capital asset pricing model, is to provide a language for discussions and negotiations. Capital markets work in mysterious ways, and we don't care if the main theories are used as descriptive approaches to understanding complex relationships. We want guidelines and turn descriptive theories - models that should be used only in search of an explanation to a phenomenon - into normative ones, i.e. models that guide our behaviour.

Approaching and studying equity markets is fascinating. Such study is driven by a strong desire to understand the market and a desire to be able to forecast price changes. The main problem is that the market is totally chaotic, and there is no easy approach to it.

The workings of the capital markets

People frequently tell me that my approach of using psychology in capital markets is really interesting, but when they hear that there is no easy solution to forecasting human reactions, they dislike it. The desire for markets to be easily and logically understood is strong and people hold on to that desire in spite of almost never being successful at investing.

The key problems with individual investing are group-think, availability bias and anchoring. These are human shortcomings that a person needs to control in order to be a better investor. Group-think, our herd instinct, is the tendency to do what the group does, and it is largely based on our desire to fit in, to be liked, to not do things that others may think odd. So, we do what others do, we accept that newspapers publish opinions from self-appointed experts who themselves have never made a profit. The challenge is to go against the group, to invest when experts say that the market is bound for depression. The challenge is to invest when markets are down and the headlines are full of negative news, and to exit when the experts are excited and ignore the short-term news and make an individual long-term investment decision based on your own opinion, carefully planned. Think how in

Warren Buffett we see a person who has not followed the herd. Availability bias means that we focus too much on what first comes to mind, what is readily available, served by our system 1. This impulse needs to be controlled, otherwise we run the risk of only investing in things that we read about or have heard mentioned.

It is only by being aware of your shortcomings as an investor that you can freely make logical decisions.

Now that we have insights into the tremendous power of myths, we need to be introduced to other hidden powers. One of the underestimated but truly strong powers that not only guides but rather controls us is our desire for belonging. This is directly related to survival and we all constantly seek our various groups or tribes; please meet neo-tribalism.

5

The Power *of* Tribalism

Many of our most influential countries are increasingly looking towards their 'glorious' pasts. In Great Britain, there is still a mental fixation around the idea of the nation as a global leader in terms of development and influence and this view is manifested in a desire to leave the European Union, to regain its former glory. When people revert back to their great history and think that the greatness will be returning, it is a system 1 search, with no or little logic. The same movement is being seen in the US and in France. When things happen around us, we look to our safe home turf. Tribalism takes over logical thinking.

Independence may be right, but it should be the fruit of logical analysis of data and review of the possibilities. In this way, the 2016 UK referendum with voters choosing to leave the EU (Brexit) has no connection to a system 2 logical search, nor has the way in which the process has been managed to date. Instead, emotions take control and when it came to the referendum it was a moment of truism; do you prefer a strong, independent and glorious UK or would you rather see our glorious history taken over by administrators in Brussels? The answer is a given system 1 answer. This is manipulation at its finest. The logical analysis is that independence comes at a high price, especially for a country that has lost most of its competitive power.

Our inner tribalistic forces can be directly traced to our past. A Darwinist perspective teaches us that social people, living together in small villages and tribes, often had a better likelihood of survival than people trying to live on their own. Being part of a tribe is a matter of survival. The tribal gene survived, and the independence gene had limited offspring. This urge for belonging may easily be seen among men, as inclusion into the hunting group was necessary for survival. Perhaps we can trace different co-operation among women, where risk monitoring and responsibility for the children was more important, but the belonging gene is equally crucial.

The concept of neo-tribalism explains that evolution has led man to survive through tribes. The ultimate expression of neo-tribalism is the fashion industry. Fashion is about taking the assumed lead in a tribal race. Alternatively, some people use fashion to make a point of not belonging, excluding themselves from the tribe. Fashion is not about innovating, it is not about what you purchase, it is rather about constantly making purchases to stay ahead and feel included in the changing trends or, if preferred, to be consciously excluded. We view people as fashionable not because they have certain clothes, but because they bought these items recently.

Tribalism received a severe shock with the arrival of industrialism, when people left the farming villages for big cities. However, the need for belonging remained strong and people joined other tribes such as football clubs, as both players and supporters, as well as bowling teams, book clubs and so on. Later, this tribe mentality began to change with the emergence of television, computers and the internet (and so on), which are all solitary activities and encourage people to stay at home. While people have been staying at home more over the last 100 or so years, the tribalistic gene has not left our DNA, so people look for other ways to belong and show the tribes they belong to. The power of our strong tribalistic urge is the main force behind marketing concepts and branding. We may be part of a European tribe, a French tribe, a Paris tribe, the Manchester United football supporters' tribe or a Rolex tribe. For instance, there is no membership per se for owning a Rolex watch, but Rolex owners may feel they are part of an invisible but powerful club; to them it has a tribalistic story based on displaying success. In the same way, we may strive to not be part of any tribe, such as a local or regional tribe, preferring to seek a more cosmopolitan or international tribe. This is also important as the borders of our countries are getting to be less important. The effect is that while our country or region-related tribal emotions are weakening, our tribalism increases in other areas, like our political affiliation or our economic status.

Our fast system 1 associations play an important part in our tribalistic desires. In fractions of seconds we create an impression of a man wearing a tailored suit, his hairstyle and glasses, and by this we create, or are offered, a view of his tribe. Similarly, we are offered clues on how we might be able to enter his particular tribe or even how to remain in our own.

One of the best examples of a modern-day tribe is Hells Angels, a global motorcycle club associated with custom-built Harley-Davidson motorcycles founded in 1948. Its critics claim that they are involved with drugs, black-mailing and prostitution and they are considered to be an organized crime syndicate by the United States Department of Justice, claims that are all denied by the Hells Angels. Irrespective of their strategy, they can be very persuasive when they show up on your doorstep. It is an international and hierarchical organization with members having to graduate to reach higher levels. Recruits will have to prove themselves over an extended period of time to be accepted. Most people fear the members of Hells Angels.

The Hells Angels are an interesting tribal phenomenon. Irrespective of their business strategy, they have managed to create a coherent organization around thousands of individuals' urges to belong. It would be difficult to find a corporation that is as successful in terms of stringent recruitment, ability to manage a diverse group of individuals that generally don't want to belong to traditional groups in society and build internal and external admiration for the brand and logo. Once in the organization, the urge to stay in and play by the rules and invisible norms is extremely powerful and will be the power serving its members with recommended system 1 decisions through the day.

The management of an organization is like any tribe and the emotional forces surrounding it will prepare and deliver recommendations during decision making processes. To be a senior manager is widely viewed similar to that of being a member of a tribe. This tribal mentality in the working environment has great implications on performance. The role of the management team is to navigate the organization's route, particularly in times of a disruptive change.

Tribalism has a strong connection to loss aversion, the cognitive bias made widely known by Daniel Kahneman, which is the tendency of avoiding losses over acquiring the equivalent as a gain. So, loss aversion turbo-charges and gives dominance to potentially negative implications over positive implications. Negative implications could be other managers not liking what we said or did, affecting our promotion chances. As a result, we second-guess what other tribe members want to hear and get in line. And with the power of system 1 being much stronger than system 2 – it's estimated to be 220,000 times stronger – we struggle to pull ourselves together, ignore the unconsciously proposed decisions and manually move into a more logical frame of mind. This means that our short-term urge to remain a member of the management tribe will dominate our ability to be a good manager or director.

Our struggle for pre-approved statements and actions is a continuous process of justification. Decision makers retrieve pre-approved external information, narratives approved by authorities and myths, and attempt to build an 'acceptable' view. The graph opposite shows how, in order to communicate in an acceptable way, management estimates based on the views of peers, rather than building and expressing their own views. The ongoing process is a form of mimicking or mimetics, a subliminal and degrading process to find out what others think. All this in order to survive.

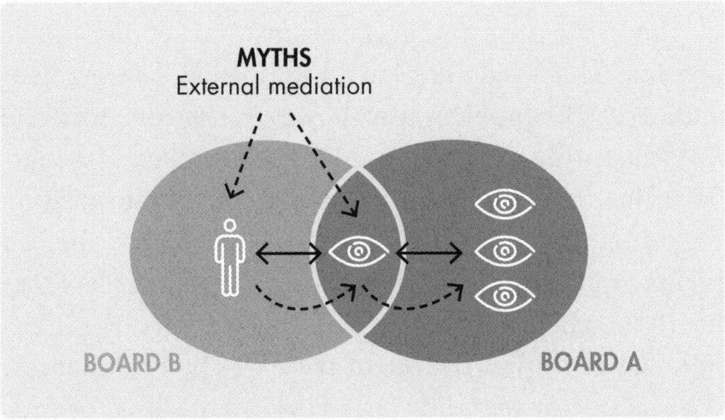

External mediation

An individual may belong to board A and as he tries to analyze the world (the curve), he estimates what his fellow director or top manager on board B thinks. He knows that the fellow is a member of board A and what they have done. So, he estimates what to say so that the fellow will be comfortable. This external mediation strongly influences us, and the forces involved are mimetics, loss aversion and tribalism.

Conducting strategic navigation of a company with crucial strategic and financial decisions often involves a balancing act between making the right investment decisions and managing risk.

There was recently a major debacle around a Swedish listed banking group. The group was formed by strong finance personalities and one of the subsidiaries had a substantial equity trading portfolio and during a period of time, the investment positions were tailor made options, which may not have had a general investment audience. The problem was, however, that the portfolio for accounting purposes needed to be valued at a market value. A single director took a contrarian position regarding the market value of the assets and as she had little support, this led her to leaving the board. The other board members apparently took the view that the internal relationship in the board tribe was more important than being transparent. When I invited the director to be interviewed in one of my classes, she reiterated that the role of the director has nothing to do with being liked by fellow directors but as a director you represent all the shareholders. This director was awarded a journalistic prize that can be translated as 'backbone of the year' for her ability to move away from making the most obvious decision and instead being able to scrutinize the decision making context and the purpose of the decision. But it is a balance – we are unable to make optimal decisions without making small compromises. Those compromises may be social: we hurt people's feelings and sometimes people just do not like us anymore. It may also be that we increase the risk of being ousted from a group or tribe. In a similar fashion, being a contrarian requires a high level of explanatory ability, so that we can win people over to our side of the story.

With regard to management, the ongoing process of increased transparency and often aggressive press coverage is fuel for tribalism. We quickly take the side that is in favour of our tribe, because the fear of being exposed makes management raise the fences and stick together. It is better to keep a low profile and not expose any potential mistakes through interviews or openness. And the more a firm is criticized, the more its tribe-members will close ranks and support each other.

There are gender aspects to tribalism. Equality is not about management teams having 50% men and 50% women. It is about everybody having the right to compete as equals. Applying system 1 and system 2 to gender equality, it is clear to see that arguing for more women to fill a quota is system 1 but applying logic to the issue and really giving it a lot of thought is system 2.

There is a famous interview with Jordan Peterson, clinical psychologist and a professor of psychology, with journalist Cathy Newman, in which Newman suggests the most obvious thought – that 50% of all CEOs in the top 100 companies should be women. This can be perceived to be passive and simple system 1 thinking, while Peterson is clearly and predominantly a hard system 2 thinker. Peterson, an excellent academic and also the author of the best-selling book, *12 Rules for Life: An Antidote to Chaos* pointed to the many variables that constitute CEO success and made it clear that although women have some of these traits, they may not be as narcissistic as is necessary. This interview was very controversial, and Peterson received a huge backlash about his comments, but perhaps as a clinical psychologist, his opinions are not to everyone's taste.

In order to have a better understanding of equality between the sexes today, we need to take a look at our evolutionary history. One view is that men have had to be creative and social to survive. This is based on the fact that, as social animals and in order to survive, humans form groups or tribes. For men, some key requirements were needed to be met for them to be recruited into successful hunting groups. So, men needed to sell themselves more as social animals. We see this when men socialize and find the need to be back-slapping and immature, fun and wild, and go on to become popular members within their groups.

There is clearly no difference in the intelligence levels of men and women and the Gaussian distribution shows this. But the graph also shows that men may be the ones on the extremes, both less clever and cleverer. See the graph opposite:

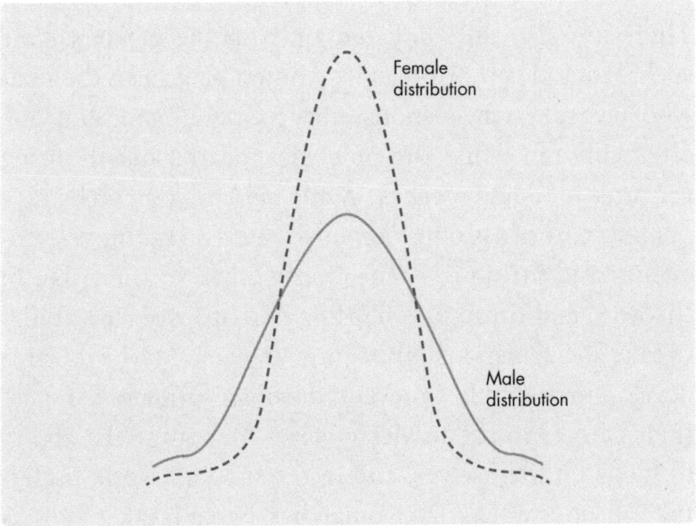

Intelligence levels example

Two distribution curves with identical means but different dispersion. Note that the curve with the greater dispersion yields higher values in both the lowest and highest ends of the range.

The same may apply to the character traits of being adventurous and creative, where on average there is no difference but, on the extremes, there is a distribution with longer tails for men. So, where does this lead us? To equality; we are all different and we need each other if we are to create equality and good performance. Equality of opportunity is truly great, but equality of outcome isn't logical, because the truth cannot be sexist.

There are also different demands on the genders. One such demand is that typically women have been the ones who have taken the responsibility to stay at home and look after children while the men disappeared into hunting ventures for days or weeks. While men focused on being a popular part of a group, women focused on taking responsibility and fitting in with other women in the tribe. In this way, and through evolution, perhaps women's ability to take social responsibility grew stronger. Maybe it is this development that has prevented women from focusing on their careers in the modern world. Men grew the ability to focus on themselves, and in the modern world undertake 70-hour weeks. Do women have what it takes to be as successful as men? The answer would off course be, 'yes'. Whilst women are different from men in many ways, it is these differences that make them suitable in their own way, such as being more agreeable, more structured and more risk-averse. All of these are excellent traits for management positions.

In the boardroom itself, the decision making process is directly affected by gender. Tribal forces are likely to make men support each other, to the detriment of good and fluent decision making. The male tribe is balanced by the board tribe, but it is unlikely that the female tribe would function in the same way. This is because often there aren't equal numbers of men and women and is also due to the pressures on women. They often make their decisions strategically and not through blind faith. Men, on the other hand, would support each other in this way.

Decision making is also affected by gender in terms of myths. There are women in the world of finance, where there appears to be little difference in terms of academic acumen. Despite this, only a fraction of people working in investment banks are women. When we look back at our evolutionary past, we can think that maybe it is not the quantitative nature of this industry that has kept women out but the requirement of deal-making attributes that need tribe inclusion. How can you get access to decision-makers if you don't have access to CEOs, mostly men, because you are not a member of the tribe, the male tribe?

Men have historically been more in power than women, so it is easy to see how agenda-setting has directly contributed to the exclusion of women. Both men and women have also contributed to keeping traditions and culture alive so it would not be right to say that it has been exclusively men who have kept women out of the boardroom; we all have, men and women alike.

Is gender equality necessary for better management decision making? Absolutely, it is clear that men are likely to take risks and that tribalism keeps women out of management positions. It is a delicate but important role of organization founders and owners to argue for the inclusion of women in such positions, because they clearly can make a difference. Likewise, it is also an important role for the chairman to mediate all decision processes so that tribalism, myths and power issues don't exclude women from being heard. This would be bad for the future and the value of any firm.

We would like to see ourselves as rational decision makers and think that it is all a matter of a cool evaluation. However, as we are, to a substantial extent, controlled by our emotions, which change depending on what is going on around us, it makes sense to study the effects of the pressure that we go through during our professional life. I have chosen to refer to this as the power of tension.

We have now been introduced to tribalism and can observe how powerful the forces that command our behaviour really are. Many people may initially see the power of myths and tribalism as weaknesses of humankind, proof that individuals can't be rational. This is correct to some extent, but we can opt to see tribalism as a way that has enabled us to survive.

Next, we will look at power issues and how the way we control and are controlled relates to our ability to make decisions.

6

The Power *of* Power

"What is your aim in philosophy?
To show the fly the way out of the fly-bottle."

Ludwig Wittgenstein

Of all the forces influencing us and our decisions, power is likely to be the most important, but equally the most difficult to grasp. This may be because it is invisible. Not only do we not see it, but we are often not aware of it. However, we can sense that people are affecting our behaviour through, for example, their body language. They may, for instance, indicate that they want a certain outcome in a discussion through their way of waving, breathing, looking at us, or by making a noise or irritated facial expression.

Sometimes people believe that just by claiming to be in control, they can enforce control. This is where successful sociopaths enter the equation – they take control and hold on to it, while the rest of us wonder what happened. Another common way is by referencing third-party authorities. These may be competitor organizations or successful individuals.

Most people are too nice to see that others are trying to control the agenda, by gradually establishing their will as the agreed route forward. Many can't see this happening and leave a meeting thinking that all parties have contributed to a successful meeting while more cunning partners leave having successfully established their agenda and plan.

Openness or weakness to being affected by the wish of another party to control us is part of system 1 thinking. The exhibition of power can start long before a meeting, when the notice of the meeting is communicated.

This is the time when the agenda is established by setting the topic and time for discussion, and material for preparation is distributed. And then, at the meeting, power can be established through the body language, the seriousness with which an issue is approached, the reaction to wishes to discuss a certain issue, and the ability to conclude the matter and close the discussion. Tools used can be an irritated voice, references to third parties, controlling the discussion and the agenda by referring to traditions and how things are normally done. Traditions are by many considered as sacred ceremonies which should not be messed with. Also, the people referring to traditions may see themselves as the judges of how well traditional procedures are followed. The control of other people in meetings is often done through careful control of the agenda and participants who don't see this coming are victims of power.

The force of power hits us from the time we are young through norms and expectations. Expectations enforce us to do well in school, be nice, find a partner and marry, and be successful in our careers. Different plays of power get us to behave according to norms of life. This is sometimes through direct instructions but can also be through indirect instructions and punishments.

Power can be seen through five different levels where the first dimension, or first face of power, is giving direct instructions to win an argument, such as when a parent tells a child what to do. This is a direct powerful command.

In the second dimension, we see power through the control of the agenda. This has a direct connection to processes in organizations where the CEO has the power to decide on the timing of topics such as strategy. This dimension where the focus is not on what is in front of you, but what has been excluded, has a direct connection to culture and traditions. Certain things like business purpose are never discussed if the environment is carefully controlled. This can also prevent management from bringing up crucial issues like new potential competitors or changing customer behaviour.

In the third dimension, the views of others are manipulated. This is the often covert and conscious strategy of calibrating mental directions so that groups that ought to have conflicting views are made to believe that the opposing view is in their own interest. This dimension has direct connections to management behaviour when some influence others consciously or unconsciously. This could be through references to processes in other competitor or larger organizations. In this respect, it is important to be aware of interconnections where some managers meet not only in the work environment under study but also in external environments. In this respect, there is a real risk of trading favours or importing processes or decisions from other companies. In the third dimension there is also a direct relation to the management through the gradual building of passive bodies created by society's and institutions' continuous and growing use of disciplinary actions. This situation is enhanced through growing transparency with decision makers becoming used to being led by authorities, rather than acting as agents for their key stakeholders.

The third dimension needs careful thought, as it is often well disguised. This is about controlling what we are doing, or even more common, what we are not doing. This is using traditions and culture as argument, while directing the focus and activities into areas where we can make people feel that they are important, while they are not allowed to deal with the things that matter.

In the fourth dimension, we are facing the group members controlling each other. There are entire societies, small towns or certain groups, where it is necessary to be accepted before you can take the lead and create change. In this case, the rule is established by the group and the tyranny over its members is exercised by the very same members. This has been referred to as mill-town or small-town culture. In the book and movie, One *Flew Over the Cuckoo's Nest*, the protagonist, Randle Patrick McMurphy tries to fight the asylum he is in from the inside and fails. Had he changed his tactic from resistance to cooperation, he may have succeeded.

This has a strong connection to the management environment, where new top managers are not allowed to force change until they have accepted the culture and the traditions of the longstanding members.

It is crucial not be a very social person, so that you can step back and not take instructions. The role of the contrarian decision maker is difficult, as it can involve being viewed as a difficult and less knowledgeable person. To stand up and demand that the process is done differently can be just what is required in order to meet the obligations as a director or manager and for the organization to be successful in the eyes of the stakeholders. It is also a matter of ethics. We need to be aware of our limited awareness to see what is going on around us and how the context of the decision making process is changing. This is referred to as bounded rationality and brings awareness to the fact that we are not equipped to be optimal decision makers. But this should not be an excuse for the absence of reflection and critical examination of our own behaviour. The process of monitoring our own and other decision makers' behaviour and how people take directions from those near the process, fellow management, is especially important as we don't consider it a problem. This is a normal effect of system 1 where we are quite content with our own abilities, without seeing what is going on.

There is one more final dimension of power play. This is the fifth dimension, reciprocity. This is where we give back if we have received something. So, if we support someone before and in the beginning of a meeting, we are more likely to get support back when we need it. The reason is that we unconsciously feel like we are partnering and becoming indebted to the person that is kind to us. Reciprocity is symmetrical and a tool to be used to control.

When we use positive reciprocity, we say positive things and create a hole, a gap or void that needs to be filled by giving back. Some people are good at creating that hole and do so in a positive way. There is also a negative reciprocity, where we say things, but they are only dressed up as something positive to demand a reply. With positive reciprocity we create a hole; with negative reciprocity, pressure is created. For instance, in some cultures, when a waiter says “enjoy!”, you are expected to reply because it would be rude not to. The implication is that the waiter in fact controls you and you are expected to reciprocate. Preparing the ground for expected responses comes very naturally to some and is a great negotiation tactic.

When learning about power-plays, the single largest threat is the invisible agenda of others. It is so easy to be seduced and, before you know what happened, be working for the other side. In the management environment, it is a challenge to not be sucked into the multitude of discussions and processes without being able to step back and review where things are coming from and where they are going. Unless you are prepared to leave the management team at any time, you will not be in the position to make changes. Dealing with power is a struggle.

We can find power-plays in the weirdest places, and it doesn’t have to be within a conscious search for control. An interesting form is the concept of taboo, something we have plenty of. This is where certain things cannot be on the agenda or, in many cases, are not even allowed to be mentioned. In the small-town cultures we often come across people who have to conform and are not allowed to say certain things. In Sweden, this is strongly pronounced through the 'Jante-law', a sort of 'I am nothing law'. It is not a real law in terms that you will be sentenced by not following it, but if you do not adhere it will be even worse, people will frown upon your behaviour and say nasty things about you. As a result, this makes it taboo to say that you have a good education, or that you think that you are clever or that you have a good salary. In a similar way, you are not allowed to say anything positive about controversial issues, such as immigration or contentious political or historical figures.

Taboos are things you are not allowed to say and are well guarded by the system 1 function of its protectors. And in the corporate world, there are lots of taboos. For example, as management should be the agents of shareholders, they shouldn't discuss the value of the company they are engaged with. Further, this is seen during severe paradigm shifts, such as digitalization, when some claim that we are not allowed to change the original purpose of the organization, because it is seen as a success. IKEA grew quickly because it managed to enable smooth transportation to people's homes and cut costs through production in low-cost countries. Although the world is changing, and we now have 3D printers which potentially could be a substitute for some of their products – it would be a taboo to question the long-term merits of flat-packed furniture among IKEA's management. Management would prove their loyalty to the soul of the IKEA organization by making this a taboo point of discussion.

In a similar manner we have a set form of corporate governance. We have directors and top management as caretakers for the wealthy shareholders who attend to corporate affairs once a year. This may have made sense in previous centuries when business environments were more stable, but in the 21st century, the world is changing so fast that a more frequent level of interaction with shareholders would benefit corporate development and achieve lower risks. Investment levels would also increase as confidence and trust would be given more room to grow. However, if you have been fostered in the current governance dogma, it is difficult to see how the main structure would be allowed to change; it would, for no real reason, be taboo to bring it up.

In the same way, the academic world is full of taboos, such as questioning academic methodology or established theories. The current generation of professors rose through the ranks using the theories on which their education was based to form their world view. It is difficult to enter the academic world with new ideas; it has been said that the academic world progresses one funeral at a time, and this may be right as some of the more radical thoughts and theories replacing paradigm myths took some 30 years from the original draft to being published. Some 97% of all articles written by ambitious academics are never published and those that are need to be edited and re-edited for some 12-18 months before being accepted by a council of peers. There is a self-preserving system and the likelihood that someone will pass through this wall of clergy is small, as is the likelihood of introducing something that goes against the grain of accepted thoughts.

There is an evident and strong link between language and strong myths; it would be taboo to verbalise anything that runs contrary to man-made myths that are upheld and guarded. So, how can one deal with taboos? You wouldn't gain anything by speaking about them. You have to gain acceptance before you build walls. The best approach in dealing with taboos is to find another type of language; find other words, find other approaches.

In the world of finance, it would not work well to say that cemented accounting principles like using historic values for pricing assets are absurd; neither would it work well to say that discounted cash flows were of no use. You may realize that CAPM is impractical and you may realize that we are fundamentally useless at forecasting, but you need to approach it through an alternative route, using a totally new approach altogether.

Adjacent to the concept of system 1 and power structures, is the understanding of the power of branding.

7

The Power *of* Branding

Brands have a direct connection to myths as being man-made constructs, something created out of thin air that we just believe in. Often it is assumed that only the marketing department should be concerned or focused on branding, and that management should be engaged or focused on more strategic issues, but you would be wrong. Branding has a direct connection with system 1 and controls the future of an organization with its customers and shareholders. So, branding is not only an issue for customers; it is just as important to get the view of potential shareholders. The perceptions and automatic responses connected to an organization's overall brand have implications for its market value as the image that the branding portrays will control the willingness of shareholders to invest or of customers to buy services or products.

With regards to shareholders, this can be referred to as financial branding. It is possible to view this kind of branding as goodwill, i.e. what we are willing to pay over and above the core net asset value. As such, it is related to how we view the value of an organization. If the value today of a future cash-flow is higher than the value of the separate assets constituting the business, the difference is the intangible asset of running the business, the goodwill of toil and imagination, the value of the brand.

Rolex watches may be one of the best-known international watch brands, and they have captured a very successful position among the other brands. Patek Philippe watches are even more expensive than Rolex watches and its advertising focuses on ownership which implies that you never actually own a Patek Philippe, you just look after it for the next generation. This image has established the Patek Philippe brand among well-educated and prosperous customers. Rolex, on the other hand, is about success. The watches are often heavy, well-built and with excellent details and craftmanship, and someone who wears a Rolex is delivering a clear message, i.e. success. The second-hand value for the most common models of Rolex: Submariner, Daytona and GMT is almost like currency, you can sell them quickly and there seems to be a steady demand. One reason is that Rolex has a steady production that doesn't give way to strong demand. If you enter the Rolex shop in Heathrow airport, they will not have the newer models, and the waiting list may be two years. This is goodwill and branding at its finest.

Branding puts every traditional thought on its head. Costs become irrelevant for Rolex and for all companies that want to concentrate on becoming valuable. The time required for Rolex to mitigate potential production costs is not well spent if instead time could be spent on exploring initiatives that will increase or generate income. So, the saying that if you look after the pennies, the pounds will look after themselves, or that you should focus on costs to increase margin, is actually wrong. The reason is simple. There is very little that you can do about the cost structure, but there is quite a lot you can do about the income structure, which can be influenced through branding. In the end, branding is more important than profit, and you can do more about your brand than your profit, so it should always be a top priority in any business.

The world is full of sound companies making a profit margin, but which are receiving no attention.

Earlier we discussed how our system 1 thinking is influenced by the power of branding with the 3Fs: fame, feeling and fluency in financial situations. Here we will explore this in more detail. The first F, Fame, refers to the positioning of an organization's name, if it is well established or if the name captures the mental space or mental capacity of others. You may see that as recognition. For example, when visiting a department store with the goal of buying soap, it is likely that you will only see the brands that you are familiar with and have seen before. This is because fame is an important factor, a recognition factor, which is irrespective of whether this is positive, negative or neutral. But the problem or shortfall of fame is that typically we only evaluate things we recognize. This is limiting and wrong and leads to cognitive biases.

The second F is for feeling. It is concerned with the emotions that are stirred in customers or shareholders when they think about the brand. The feelings evoked are again based on system 1 thinking and it takes a lot of effort to circumvent our automatic responses. Feeling negative towards something cannot easily be overcome. An example is an unnamed Swedish bank that had a contrarian and outspoken chairman. He may generally be right but certain statements don't go well with journalists in a small-town culture. This may have created negative perceptions of the bank, resulting in fewer investors ready to consider it as a good investment opportunity.

This hurts the bank's market valuation compared with peers. The equity analyst would like to think that this has a logic, but even with these quantitative people, their system 1 has 220,000 times more power than their logical side and as their unconscious system 1 ranks the investment alternatives, the system 2 has to work hard to find and manipulate the evidence needed to deliver investment proposals.

The third F is for fluency, the ability to find distinct differences between various options; which in turn leads to the ability to make decisions. Managers searching for value in their products and for their stock should work on the distinctiveness, or they are investing in a way which will benefit other similar brands.

The former CEO of German automobile manufacturer Audi, Franz-Josef Paefgen, believed that the mission of branding should be to deliver a promise. He believed that it is not the technology of a product that invokes the 3Fs in customers, but the art and positive intuition, which can be described as goodwill, which encourages customers to make the financial investment.

When the Italian luxury shoe company Tod's invested in cleaning and restoring the Colosseum in Rome in 2018, it was building its brand into a paradigm myth, a man-made construct that is difficult to erase. How can you go against Tod's when they are part of Roman history?! With this initiative, Tod's is building a reputation and showing that it cares about Italy and Italians, it is associating itself with its followers and customers. However, what happens when an organization moves from one market to another, such as when Jaguar Land Rover, a British automotive company, moved the production of its iconic range, the Range Rover to India? Everything became more fragile and the 3Fs of the brand became less sustainable, creating a shortcut to lower value.

As shown by these examples, in any industry it is important for organizations to be seen to be engaged in numerous markets (see graph page 122). The following points should be noted:

1. Apart from the product or service the company is focusing on, the strategic position it has in a particular market is important.

2. For many companies, the capital market would be as important or more important as it takes time to build the position that may be needed in the future.

3. Many companies are in a competitive market for talent. In a constantly changing context where there are various forms of disruption, hiring can be crucial for survival and success.

4. The company is dependent on its suppliers, receiving key products and business intelligence, which is also a market position to be guarded.

5. Lastly, all employees and various stakeholders such as brand ambassadors are a key group.

So, which market is most important? The answer is that they all are, because branding and reputation are interconnected. The organization that only focuses on its product market will be less attractive in the capital markets and the value will suffer. Ignoring the fact that shareholders are also customers, potential employees and suppliers may seem to make for strategic decisions, but this may result in bad reviews from the press and the employees. Where is the value going? Down.

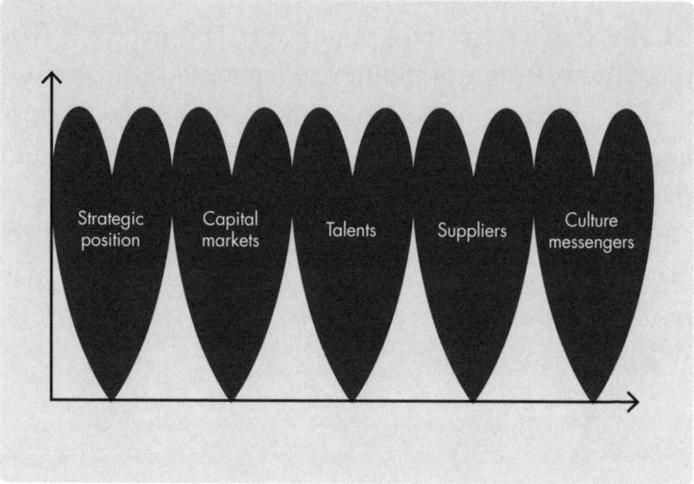

Which market is most important?

All of them are. In any industry it is important for organizations to be seen to be engaged in numerous markets.

Reputation gained through branding is seen by many as less relevant because capital markets and analysts are rational. The fact is that analysts and investment managers have little control over their decisions. Although they are often well-paid to make logical decisions, they are just as exposed to system 1 passive thinking as anyone else. In fact, it is often likely that an analyst makes a decision, and then works hard to find the evidence to support it.

The behaviour of analysts can be compared to that of potential voters before an election. Election polls are often useless as people are more likely to indicate politically correct views in polls, while when it comes to real voting, they see the seriousness of the situation, move from system 1 into system 2 and give their real view. In fact, it would make more sense if a researcher that wants to predict the outcomes of an election were to ask people how they think their neighbours will vote. This question is quite indirect, and a more truthful answer is likely to be given.

So, what are the implications for myths, tribalism and the power of branding? They all contribute to passive decision making, our system 1. It is important to understand and appreciate that we lean on myths and man-made constructs because the truth may be complicated and affect the view the world has of our brand. And in a similar way, tribalism, our need for belonging or our distaste for a certain tribe, may have a direct effect on the future of organizations, chosen risk levels and corporate market value.

In the final example for this chapter, we will consider the Scandinavian bank Nordea with its outspoken former Chairman Björn Wahlroos. Mr. Wahlroos, who can be considered both a contrarian and a logical decision maker, has made statements that, although clever and certainly true, have met resistance from journalists and the bank's reputation is likely to have suffered. The views of management may have been the result of financial myths, such as the decision to move the head office from Stockholm to Helsinki, a cost-saving decision. However, it is likely that the dynamic effects on reputation and branding have not been included in the financial considerations.

Similarly, the decision to purchase an expensive apartment for the CEO may have reputational effects after having been negatively represented in the newspapers. With such actions, it is not only myths that come in to play, but also tribalism; people who have Nordea shares may see themselves as a part of the same tribe that makes bold and 'capitalistic' decisions.

In conclusion, it is difficult for most people to fathom how important branding is and how we are affected by brands. We normally don't recognize how we are affected by the immense power of branding, but our entire perception, our responses, are the sum of someone's branding efforts. However, there are other forces in play.

Our immediate responses, with a simple, fast solution, enable us to survive. Through the study of our past we can understand the traits that enabled some to survive and reproduce. Our roles required different things from us depending on whether we are male or female. We have to address the power of tension.

8

The Power *of* Tension

Tension has a direct link to system 1 and short-term versus long-term decision making. Tension occurs when pressure builds as a result of conflicting narratives or when we are being informed of something that we disagree with. In organizations we often see tension when strategy discussions are in conflict with our perception of the organization and where it should be going. How we deal with tension depends on our personalities.

Tension is like pain, so when we experience tension, we become uncomfortable and try to resolve the situation as soon as possible, to get rid of the pain. In these situations, we tend to become agreeable and go along with things, unless they are totally off, so that we can go back to a tensionless state. Trying to depart from tension is a system 1 reaction. We see the solution that will get us out of the tension and may make the decision regardless of it being the right or the wrong one.

The decisions required to steer organizations well in the long term are often painful and full of tension. But if we are unable to sustain tension, and choose the easy way out, we may navigate the organization towards agreeableness and short-term gains. In such cases, we are not doing our job.

There are people that have the ability to use tension to their advantage to drive the outcomes that they desire. By building tension around one issue and showing others how to get rid of the tension and take the easy way out, they are in fact manipulating people to their advantage.

Just as we smoke despite knowing it is dangerous in the long run and we eat too many unhealthy foods, we let system 1 carry us into the easy, short-term solutions. Similarly, tension is a great server of system 1 solutions and those who are aware of this will create strategic and social tensions and so control decision making.

It is easy to assume people that argue are certain about their view and their position on matters. But there are times when people create tension because they are, in fact, uncertain. And arguing can be an unconscious way to verify something that you are actually uncertain about. Tension can be used to lead a person out of system 1, because in this state we are passive and are open to making the easy decision (to do what is suggested), or to being forced to consciously think.

But tension can be good too. The process of innovation can often be a result of tension; you have to come up with a solution, so you muster all your available resources to find one. Although this is an uncomfortable state, something good can come out of it. For instance, when a person is fired from their job, the tension created at that moment may force the person to see this as an opportunity to become an entrepreneur.

Tension can cause discomfort and, as is human nature, we try to avoid things that hurt us. With this in mind, we need to understand that tension is a sign of change, of potential for development and the chance to move into something better. So, when tension is experienced, you should not look for the easiest way out, that would be giving into a comfortable state where you in fact don't contribute anything. On the other hand, if tension is experienced because things are going well, but there is no resistance or progress, it may be that you are surrounded by the wrong people. In order to progress, you need clever people and if you find that you are the smartest person in the room, you need change to another room. Substitute the people for others or leave. To create and maintain any kind of transformation, you have to facilitate change by putting a new team in place. This is because when employees have been together for too long, they become set in their ways and a culture that prevents change is cemented. It is also important to bear in mind that we adjust to the company we keep; in fact, individually we become the average of the five people we spend most of our time with. You need to surround yourself with clever people, so it is best not to recruit people like yourself, but instead to recruit better people, smarter people, contrarians, people that don't necessarily fit in.

Some people are less popular because they tend to create tension, for example Donald Trump. These individuals typically make decisions that others in their position would not make. In the first instance, this creates tension, but it also makes people react and forces them to review possible strategic routes they had not previously considered. Trump rattles cages and forces people into new positions, for many an uncomfortable system 2 position. But Trump is a contrarian and doesn't appear to care that people don't like what he is doing.

In politics, there is a fine line between creating a state of tension and doing things that avoid getting into areas that are painful. It is a different consideration for decision makers in organizations, because decisions can make or break a company. In these situations, it is important to break with tradition, threaten a stale culture and get close to a long downward slope in order to make the necessary changes.

We are to a large extent controlled by how we see ourselves and our organization – where we come from, where we are now and where we are going. When this perspective changes, we may feel cognitive dissonance. This hurts and we seek correction as quickly as possible. In the next chapter, the power of narrative is explained.

9

The Power *of* Narrative

Our narratives are the stories we see with ourselves as the starring character. They are the source of many conflicts and misunderstandings. Our narrative is how we position ourselves in the present, but it is based on our history and where we are going. Our chain of narratives undergoes constant change as we adapt our history and our future; it needs to fit together and to be in harmony. If this is not the case, we have narrative conflicts.

Narratives are about system 1 thinking. Unless we try to program ourselves into something different, our narratives have a strong presence as a guiding path along which we live our lives. And if something clashes, we may have to go into a state of tension where we gradually recalculate and adjust our narrative.

In the graph below, we see two people and how they view their past, present and future. Everything is totally flexible:

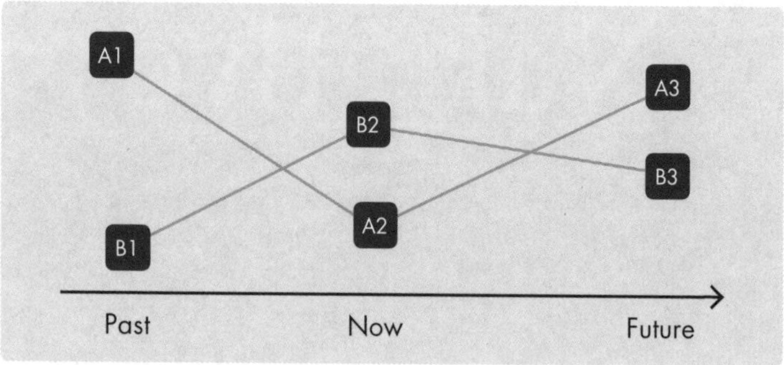

Narratives

How two people, A and B, view the past, present and future.

People are in the present but can visualize their past and their future, and all stages need to fit together. If something happens when you are in a harmonious relationship between past, present and future, whereby the future looks less achievable, we can end up in a narrative conflict. Examples could be when we lose a job or find out that our partner has had an affair. Our narrative looks less achievable and we get angry.

a. **Adjustment of the past.** We can adjust how we view our past to fit in with the current view of ourselves and where we are going. This can mean creating an oppressed narrative, i.e. the reason that we are where we are today is because someone has been mean and hurt our chances for a brighter future. However, I have a relative who changed his narrative in a more positive way. He had always been poor but inherited some money and is now quite well off. He doesn't like his past narrative, so he has changed it to align with his current narrative. He doesn't want to see the inheritance as his source of wealth, and instead sees himself as having come from a good family and the money as having always been there. It's a nice narrative.

   In a similar way, we have the successful entrepreneur, who likes to enhance his standing by convincing people that he built his firm based on careful business intelligence and clever strategies, but when we do our own analysis, we can see how he, based on the information available, made all the wrong choices. He was just lucky – not a narrative you want to brag about.

b. **Adjustment of present situation.** We can see the politician with a firm hold on his past narrative and a romantic view of himself in the future; the hero that is remembered for his good deeds and his clever decisions. However, there are negotiations to be made and he will need to be politically astute. So, he needs to be flexible and make compromises.

c. **Adjustment of the future.** It is common to adjust the vision of a future narrative so that the present feels comfortable. This could be communicating to the surrounding world that you have a vision or objective that enables the current lack of success to appear as actual intent. Watering down the success that is sought in the future makes one's control of one's life and the present seem more comfortable.

There are different kinds of narratives that provide good tools for analyzing the structure in which we operate. Some of them are:

a. **Oppressed narrative.** "We feel miserable and it is your fault." Saying this sort of thing doesn't make us feel better but it allows us to put the blame on somebody else. This is pure system 1 thinking as it makes each decision easier and we can lead contented lives, not having to deal with the tension of taking charge of our situations and changing our lives. The oppressed narrative gives us the opportunity to feel better by looking miserable, so long as we can blame somebody else.

b. **Clever narrative.** This is the positioning of yourself as very clever. You do well because you are very talented. Another way of glorifying your cleverness is by saying that the reason your performance is somewhat mediocre is that you never study, you never do your homework because you don't have to, you are so clever, so you do alright anyway. These people usually end up in a mess once they talk their way into difficult university classes, where they fail. They were not that clever after all.

c. **Offended narrative.** People who use the offended narrative, a complex power route to making you feel guilty, bask in their own failure and try to climb on you to make them feel better, to feel some sort of achievement from people allowing them to be miserable. Offended narrative differs from the oppressed narrative in that is more related to the present – the focus is on looking offended. Oppressed narrative is taking a position of historically being oppressed and therefore having a tough time today.

d. **Happy family narrative.** "And you may find yourself in a beautiful house; with a beautiful wife; and you may ask yourself, well, how did I get here?"*. This is a large area in that it is about peoples' existence and the meaning of life. People grow up and walk straight into relationships and marriage without ever pausing

Note Taken from *Once in a Lifetime*, song by David Byrne and Talking Heads band from their "Remain in Light" studio album.

and questioning their own direction and motives. Then they wake up to reality but may not dare to doubt their own route and destiny. We all want to be liked and to be successful, but we can't all have, say, successful careers. However, we can reach something that is difficult for others to check and verify: we can build a happy family. I think this is a tricky and sensitive end-goal for a lot of people in the sense that it must be right, and if it isn't, then what purpose is there in life? I often hear people saying that they are part of a tight, happy family. It comes down to existentialism and neo-tribalism where people are looking for meaning and belonging. It is a good escape route for someone looking for meaning and is something that we aren't allowed to question. This is a narrative used by a lot of people who are not necessarily parts of really happy families.

e. **Poverty narrative.** This could be a way of glorifying your own position in life by positioning yourself with very humble beginnings, that everything you have achieved is because you are very able. To some extent it is the opposite of the oppressed narrative. You are not blaming anybody; you are basking in your own ability.

f. **Heritage narrative – class narrative.** We can understand the successful Patek Philippe advertisement implying that you are doing well, you were born into money and were given an expensive watch, and now you plan to pass on that watch to your kid. This is status and system 1 thinking. We admire old money because we intuitively associate it with class. This is a great narrative if you can pull it off.

g. **Macho narrative.** This is an easy position to take where, through showing that you are a real brute who drives motorcycles, climbs hilltops, lifts weights or has the beard and the tattoos, you prove that you have arrived in a comfort zone and nobody should challenge you.

h. **Tribal narrative.** A tribal narrative could be the substitution of a successful group for your own mediocre success. Think Manchester United: the fact that you are part of their tribe makes you equally successful – what you live for is the tribe and you can feel successful as nothing else than the success of the team matters. The key seems to be the importance of belonging, of being successful at belonging, that is, a tribe narrative.

i. **Intellectual narrative.** We see this on campus where it is acceptable to dig deep down into research issues or enrich the world with academic success. It is a great lifestyle to link up to a higher calling and if you have glasses and untidy hair, the narrative is getting close to being complete. Both a lifestyle and a narrative.

j. **Acquirer narrative.** In terms of making corporate acquisitions, we can fall into the trap of having a conqueror's narrative where we allow ourselves to bask in the glory of having won, having defeated an organization by buying them. This is a system 1 feeling while the correct perspective would be to see the challenge, go into a system 2 mood and try to retain any financial value left after the transaction.

k. **Acquired narrative.** Although what is trying to be achieved is a merger, the legal transaction is an acquisition. Staff of the acquired company could feel like losers, like they have been conquered.

l. **Huge and growing narrative.** With corporate narratives, we build a corporate story around where we've been, where we are and where we are going. Our company's history becomes the crucial key for our clients and employees to understand who we are.

m. **Entrepreneurial narrative.** We see people calling themselves serial entrepreneurs and our system 1 minds assume this is something good. The right question may be that if you are that good an entrepreneur, why do you have to start and re-start so many companies? The most successful entrepreneurs bask in the glory of their success, which no doubt takes both intelligence and hard work. If you reach the pinnacle of entrepreneurship, you then start giving away money. Then you are not only successful, you become god-like when you are so good that you give away everything that you have made. This is a great narrative which may be the ultimate driving force, creating a legacy.

n. **Marxist narrative.** Marxism is mostly about substituting individual rights with the power of the group. A Marxist narrative would work head on against capitalism which places individual ability first. A Marxist narrative is a romantic story about equality. The main problem with the narrative is the Pareto principle, that people generally have various levels of intelligence and drive and there will always be a fraction of people that do better, that become leaders and make more money.

o. **Capitalist narrative.** By placing certain countries, certain people and certain politics in a capitalist narrative, people can remove perceived qualities from other people and countries.

p. **Political party narrative.** Sweden managed to build a high standard of living for its citizens by staying out of the great wars and fostering a relationship between capitalism and a socialistic state. This has fostered a certain culture and traditions which are becoming increasingly exposed to international economic forces. Still, many people, including the largest political party, the social democrats, have difficulties in changing their historic platform for decision making and can't cooperate with parties deemed to be capitalistic. They appear to see it as a betrayal to deviate from their future narrative, "the safe home for everybody". This gets in the way of progress. This is to some extent also related to power issues meaning that change is not allowed to be on the agenda by senior party officials.

q. **Tenure narrative.** Career academics that need to get permanent employment often need to publish in peer-reviewed journals. This creates a mimetic form of performance; aspiring professors write things that are likely to become published. The intention to get tenure will control research activities and the development of science. It will also prevent cross-functional development.

r. **Corporate narrative.** We have a view of what a company is, with consideration to its history and its future. This is an unconscious process but it is a part of our corporate decisions. When this involves strategic decisions, we find ourselves controlled by traditions and culture, a behaviour related to our reluctance to change and system 1 thinking.

s. **Governance narrative.** A limited liability company structure with annual meetings of shareholders and a board have been and continue to be a successful structure supporting investments, growth and control. We see the board of directors as having responsibility for strategy, leaving operations to a CEO. The board is elected annually by the shareholders, the supreme stakeholder group. This perspective is to a large extent a legacy of Milton Freedman and we may need to look at alternative narratives if we want to make the best of our endeavours. This may mean that corporations should be operated for the benefit of several groups of stakeholders, not only shareholders, and that directors need a closer and more frequent

> contact with shareholders and other stakeholder groups. In addition, with increasing complexity and simultaneous transparency and personal liability, other forms of governance promoting professional insight may be needed.

The study of conscious decision making leads towards existential issues. When we study ourselves, where we are, where we have been and where we are going, it is difficult for many to choose a road less travelled. Many people believe that carving a new future which differs from what everybody else in their family has done is insurmountable and prefer to follow a typical narrative. As such, this narrative is powerful. It becomes more difficult to actively vote against following the narrative than to follow it: saying no to doing what everybody else is doing becomes a conscious system 2 decision. We prefer to end up in situations that we are familiar with, situations that are similar to those of others around us. We may end up with a partner, two or three children, a Volvo and a Labrador dog without knowing at all how we got there. This drive to do what feels natural is what enabled us to survive as a species, but it is also this force that makes us less efficient in many ways.

A good example is shown in the book *Of Human Bondage* by W. Somerset Maugham. This is the story of Philip Carey, who spends a large part of his life in search of a role, a narrative with which he can be content. In the end, it all becomes very simple when Philip realizes that the meaning of life is that "the simplest pattern – that in which a man was born, worked, married, had children, and died – was likewise the most perfect." The ultimate message from *Of Human Bondage* perfectly captures system 1 thinking – we should let others decide what is good, rather than searching within ourselves and making up our own minds based on our own desires.

In another example we can see that when a person's narrative changes, the change can be difficult for others to understand or accept. The Swedish soccer player Zlatan Ibrahimović went through an unusual transformation from being a teenager in Sweden who was skilled in playing soccer to becoming Sweden's best soccer player and perhaps one of the best soccer players in Europe. Along the way, Zlatan's narrative had to change from the one that was confined to a Swedish town culture. Zlatan made a lot of money as a professional soccer player and developed new habits and new visions of success; he became involved in products carrying his name and earned additional income from advertisements. The new narrative, that soccer is a means for becoming a wealthy businessman, did not match the previous narrative where soccer was seen primarily as a form of social engagement that creates enjoyment for others and supports clubs and activities for young people. Changes can happen in all kinds of situations, personal and professional, and they are the fruit of changing narratives.

Taking control of our destiny involves making non-choices into choices. It involves being prepared to be considered the odd one out, the contrarian one, and as a result not being very popular. Taking control of our destiny involves making decisions consciously, decisions that relate to narratives; changing our narrative from something that is just there into something that we shape according to our own will. This involves taking a step back, spending the time to really think through what we need to do. Some of us can think well while doing something else, i.e. while walking or driving. For others, we need to do nothing else – just close our eyes and think of our future.

While we may pay tribute to the importance of narratives, we seldom consider them as a tool for aligning management and assisting the company in reaching its potential value. An ongoing example is where people's views of the company's future position and strategic intent differ. While one person may look at the business as gaining success through acquisitions and organic growth, another person may see that the industry will be disrupted by new types of market alternatives and substitutions will change the company radically. Either way, the differing perspectives on what the company will be like in the future and therefore the activities in which the company currently should engage in will differ radically. In fact, two participants may end up arguing and feeling substantial tension, and the company will suffer, without seeing the root cause.

A solution may be to investigate further the original culture of the company, the hidden and clear intentions among the key stakeholders and then thoroughly discuss various narrative alternatives and then try to agree on one way forward. This is directly related to business strategy, but it makes sense to let the strategy follow from a widely agreed business narrative.

The aim of the previous chapters has been to get the tools to make better decisions. The expectation is that when we have those tools, when we climb the ladder to a better understanding, when we are not as easily swayed by what others say, we can make better decisions. The next chapter gives a perspective on the way of doing so.

10

Making Important Decisions

"We usually think of ourselves as sitting in the driver's seat, with ultimate control over the decisions we make and the direction our life takes; but, alas, this perception has more to do with our desires – with how we want to view ourselves – than with reality."

Dan Ariely

Part of the strong grip the group has on its members is shown by how members have difficulties in seeing what is going on inside the group. It takes an outsider to see it. Likewise, it takes someone from outside of business administration to be able to successfully scrutinize the management behaviour. Daniel Kahneman contributed to the excellent article "Before you make that big decision", which I have used in the classroom for years and which has helped many students to understand cognitive weaknesses more fully. This article is used here as a structure for a pre-decision process.

At times when management is getting closer to making decisions, the following points should be considered:

1. Group-think
2. Confirmation bias
3. Halo effect
4. Sunk cost bias
5. Loss aversion
6. Disaster neglect
7. Availability bias
8. Saliency bias
9. Heuristic affects
10. Self-interested bias
11. Anchoring bias
12. Overconfidence
13. Tribalism
14. Myths
15. Power
16. Narratives
17. Gender and diversity
18. Mimetic behaviour

Group-think

Review the risk of being a part of group-think. This may be when we get sucked into the movement of the group, when everybody is excited and there aren't any dark clouds on the horizon. Groups easily turn into sects and just as with some religious sects, people change their views after having left the group. This is by definition difficult, but an approach may be to review the project as a pre-mortem position. That is, if you try to imagine yourself reviewing your company or the project at hand in a few years and it has all failed miserably. What caused the failure? What caused the problem? The advantage is that in this position the few gnawing potential problems that you may be aware of, but you didn't allow to surface nor had the chance to be discussed, come out. In the stream of group-think, where everything is rosy, it may be too difficult and socially unacceptable to bring up potential problems, but if you can move the process into another room where the failure is more acceptable and evident, new things are allowed to be discussed. In the boardroom, where you have the responsibility to represent thousands of stakeholders, you cannot consciously be seduced into the movement of the group: you need to resist. You need to step back and take the time to review, reconsider and study the logic and alignment with corporate purpose of what you are about to support. In the case of a dividend decision, it is easy to follow your fellow decision makers and feel the excitement about being able to report yet another increase, but is this really prudent, or are we just being populist, risking the cash position of and thereby the future of the company?

Confirmation bias

This weakness is inherited from our hunting past and means that we need to focus on opportunities. So, when looking for evidence for our position, we are likely not to see things that are contrary to our assumed position. Checking for confirmation bias is to some extent about spotting group-think in other groups, for example the management group. Management may lean heavily on advisors such as bankers and auditors, but it is always better to look at a problem from a completely different viewpoint, to listen to advice from people who do not have a history with the company, and who have a lot less or nothing to lose.

Halo effect

We have a cognitive weakness when we assign abilities to somebody that is verifiably strong in other areas. For instance, we are prone to listen more to good-looking people because system 1 likes them more than unattractive individuals. In the same manner, we may promote an excellent CFO to the position of CEO because of his or her abilities in accounting and finance and because he or she is good in these areas, and we have respect for their views in strategy and management. However, they may not have been the right person for the job. Again, the ability to step back and contemplate alternative decisions could be important. The halo effect may be one of the big mental weaknesses of management.

Sunk cost bias

We often feel like we have invested so much in a project that we can't stop the process. With regard to investments, this is when we have placed money into something that turns out to be a mistake, but we find it too hard to take the consequences, so we postpone the pain by keeping it alive, by investing a bit more. It may be useful to reflect on any situation and ask yourself the question that if you were faced with the original investment proposition today, with the knowledge you have now, would you make the investment? If the answer is no, drop the project. Sunk cost bias has a strong connection to mental accounts where you place your assets and liabilities in several obscure accounts where they cannot be compared in a transparent way. It is important to realize that it is the process of change that is the problem, regardless of any specific asset you have.

Loss aversion

Are we being logical about comparing risks and rewards or have we just exaggerated the pain associated with the downside in comparison to the fortunes of the upside? This may be the perfect role in assisting management to properly evaluate the merits of a project.

Disaster neglect

Nassim Taleb introduced the concept of black swans – just because certain risks have a low probability doesn't mean they should be ignored. If they actually materialize, they could drag your entire firm down with them. The direct connection to confirmation bias is that while people involved in the process only see supporting arguments, they similarly cannot see potential big disasters. This could include the risk of an important partner failing, funding disappearing or laws changing.

Availability bias

There is a direct link to system 1, as availability bias is about our thoughts having been prepared and served to us without our conscious permission. For example, if we have seen pictures from airplane crashes, we may remember these images when considering travelling options and choose to travel by car despite widely available statistics showing that being on the roads is far more dangerous than being in the air. Daniel Kahneman said that nothing is as important as when we think about it. We aren't able to control the free float of our thoughts and the amount of mental capacity they take.

Saliency bias

This is the fight between system 1 and 2, and as we quickly make connections between various aspects of things, we often make poor connections as well. When we review an investment, we risk making comparisons with other successful projects because they are in the same industry or because they have people, regions or even names in common with us. In this case, we need to be contrarian and review the project from another angle. If another project in a similar industry was successful, was this because of the industry or because of its management, culture and strategy, and is a comparison with our project really relevant?

Affect heuristic

This has a strong connection to group-think and confirmation bias as we may get so excited with the merits of the project and the potential outcome that we are unable to see any weaknesses. Step back, delay decision making and revisit the project without this initial excitement.

Self-interest bias

What are the stakes of management in the proposed decision? In the case of a dividend, is management recommending that funds are maintained in the company and used for investment to enhance its position? A review of a decision from this angle may reveal a conflict of interest that is suboptimal for other stakeholders.

Anchoring bias

This is when an evaluation or analysis has used certain numbers and the use of other assumptions shows a different outcome. Anchoring is a weakness as certain numbers may stick, and we can't force ourselves to reconsider the basic assumptions. In negotiations one party may throw in a number early to establish a level where they would like the final agreement to end up. The other party may need to ignore the bait and analyze the project without the bias the other party tried to establish. In the workplace this may mean ignoring irrelevant arguments such as people referring to traditions or previous levels.

Overconfidence

We generally like confident people, as we like success. However, in a management context where we have accepted responsibility for other people's money, it is not good enough to rely on another member's confidence to decide. Prudent behaviour is to look at verifiable data and do our own analysis of statistical information and, after that, estimate what the future holds.

Tribalism

Tribalism is closely related to identity and roles. Can we see which groups have the strongest 'pull' on the people involved? Although they may be 'our' management team, the members may feel closer to other groups, including our counterparty in negotiations. Remember that we are easily seduced and that we belong to many overlapping tribes. It may be that the people who are introducing the background to the decision required or who are participating in the decision making process with you are subject to avoiding loss and are more concerned with continuing to be a part of the group instead of making the right decision for all stakeholders. But will this have a bearing on the decision being made? Are those involved approaching the decision at hand from a correct perspective or are they saying things that they think people from their tribe, or desired tribe, want to hear?

Myths

Do we fully understand the theories we refer to, or do we have a distorted view of those – something that could be guiding us incorrectly? Many theories are difficult to grasp, but because we are familiar with them and may find them comforting, we don't attempt to challenge their assumptions. This is particularly the case for financial theories. Most business managers come into contact with financial theories when they go to business schools and are expected, if you are a general decision-maker in a business, to know things like the cost of capital or calculating the return on an investment. As myths are simplifications of more complex matters, there is substantial reason to challenge these theories – in particular if they are not properly understood by everybody, which is almost always the case. Beware of people using the complexity of theories as a tool to get their viewpoint across.

Power

If we review the decision making process we are a part of, can we see individuals who may have controlled the agenda or who are safe-keepers of traditions and rituals? It is difficult but of crucial importance to be able to step away and critically review the process at hand. Are there people using power-tools to control our behaviour? It is important to realize that some people have the ability to get the support of others and collectively go against anyone who has the guts to question a process. Watch out for people that try to control their surroundings through their body language; it could be a form of management through fear – 'don't you dare to contradict me now'. People using power can ruin a company and it is the chairman that is responsible for arranging an orderly process where the power issues are minimized.

Narratives

Narratives are the stories that people assume they are part of. They are powerful, as an entire issue or perspective can be placed within a fundamental narrative. In relation to a corporate narrative, this could be the purpose of the company and the industry. It can be that management are the agents of only the owners, or that directors and managers should act for all the stakeholders. In terms of management, should we see them as acting in their own interests and does that mean that there are different objectives among management and directors? Are the people involved positioning the decision in a particular narrative? This could be that our peer companies are going a certain way or that there are certain expectations among stakeholder groups. Do you agree with the chosen narrative? Remember that profitability as an objective is a narrative and it is not certain that it is the right narrative as agreed among the stakeholders.

Gender and diversity

It is of crucial importance to check if there are gender or diversity issues at hand in the decision. Are we giving everybody the chance to be heard or are we excluding certain individuals or issues in the decision at stake? Discriminating is part of system 1 thinking, so we have to use our system 2 to critically review the reasons for certain proposals and the way certain decision processes are going.

Mimetic behaviour

Social pressure and the avoidance of conflicts often make us avoid controversial statements. I often notice that people don't even communicate through exchanging words, they just dance along and say things that they know the other person is about to say. People actually think they are having a real conversation. The power of system 1 makes us say things that we can figure out will be right and true for the people listening in. Some people say things such as "it is better to have a good strategy than a bad one", or, "it makes more sense to be careful when we make this acquisition than being careless". People that say these things are quite useless, there is no room for them in a company at any level.

Going through this list of points and comparing the applicability of each with the decision at hand may result in issues that need to be checked and resolved. By doing the exercise, trying to move into a conscious system 2 context, you are getting closer to serving your stakeholders.

When you are able to contribute to making better decisions without being affected by the weakness and power-attempts of others, you become resilient and sustainable and of more value to your employer and society.

11

The Contrarian Statesman

"Like a homeless person staying behind in a bar with the chairs on the table – everyone has left and he just sits there like he doesn't understand."

Ulf Lundell

Our social skills are hard-coded into our body. It is a challenge for most people with social ambitions to go against the convictions of other people. While there are ways of cleverly going about it, the risk is that if you don't follow the flow of system 1, if you don't buy into the myths, stick to the tribe or obey the power-plays of others, you will be deemed to be a difficult person. One has to ask first if it is worth it.

The right answer may be that it depends on the purpose of your social relations. I have found myself in casual and social relationships where I wish I had not been so difficult. I remember a particular instance where my wife and I were hiking with some friends. At the time I happened to be reading *Thinking, Fast and Slow* for the third time, which led me to gradually come to the view that I was surrounded by shallow and not very intelligent individuals. There was a particular discussion, quite a trivial one about the content of a type of drink, where I knew I was in the right, but the discussion was not going my way. In the end I felt that I had had enough and not only took a contrarian position, but I did so in a challenging way. That dinner ended with me leaving my friends and wife and going to my room. I realized that I was being childish and that I have to separate serious matters from purely social matters. This was not the time to be clever and smart. This was an opportunity to be an adult and let things pass. I realized that it is clearly better to remain married than to be a contrarian.

However, it is different in management positions. One needs to understand the reasons why management have been appointed to the position and let reason guide and drive a contrarian behaviour:

1. **The purpose of the company.** The objective of the company is normally to make money but is this for the short run or long run? Are there other matters that should be influential?

2. **The wishes of the shareholders.** This is a key area but the one where I see that management generally could do a much better job. Ask stakeholders what they want and ask shareholders if they want dividends or their funds in the company reinvested. CEOs should meet shareholders every month. What could be more important than listening to your owners and taking in their views and wishes?

3. **The law.** This is the easy part. To follow the law is easy as long as the management are not trying to become too clever or greedy for their own good.

4. **The devil's advocate.** It may be that the decision making process could benefit the role holder, but the person that takes a reflective and critical position, that doesn't go with the flow, may be in a better position to see where the strategy and the decision process are taking the organization. It may also be necessary to watch out for power-plays within the management team.

To take a contrarian perspective may mean considering doing exactly the opposite of what is about to be decided or the opposite of how things are done normally. This may require both strength and imagination. Consider what would be the likely outcome or what the worst possible reaction would be. Sometimes there is value in shaking things up. It may also be useful to not show everybody where one is going. Sometimes, in order to turn left, you first need to turn right. When practicing martial arts, you don't push in the obvious direction first, you shake up the balance of your competitor by pushing in the direction that is least expected.

With system 1, there is often a stream of group-think as we get closer to a decision point. By conveying through body language and facial expressions that the proposed solution is the best, the colleague driving the decision shows that by agreeing with them there is the future potential of reciprocity, and so most people go with the flow and take the easy way out, thinking about the social consequences of saying no. They go along. One way to act against this may be to line up all the principles and criteria together with the information at hand and draw up alternative solutions, and then include the totally different solutions, the one that a contrarian would be proud of. It is of crucial importance to realize that system 1 serves us and most others with the same alternatives, and this is why we behave like lemmings, running toward the same solution. Doing what everybody else does may not necessarily create value. On the contrary, being able to see the system 1 behaviour of others (including competitors) can be used as a resource for building a better value for your firm through steps such as the following:

1. Getting out of the market
2. Shrinking the organization
3. Splitting the business
4. Merging with unequals
5. Leveraging up
6. Changing crew

Getting out of the market

In the case of a strategic decision, this means lining up all the obvious competitors and what they are doing. It means studying their annual reports and in particular strategy documents by the CEOs. However, another route could be to look at the companies that supply substitute or alternative services to your customers – are these companies in fact sliding closer to your business? Is this space getting crowded? One contrarian decision would be not to invest but to divest; to look at the value of your market position for others and let them bid against each other and pay a premium. The funds you receive may be the highest price ever paid in the industry and others may envy your decision of getting out early. So, you get your top price and then you can watch others piling into the already crowded space. You have now been resilient to system 1, you have taken a step back, reflected and taken a decision which is contrary to what others are doing.

Shrinking the organization

In order to expand and grow your business, your top line is a generally accepted way of building value. As your income grows faster than your costs, the profit in absolute terms gets larger and the firm becomes more valuable. Size is also important: as you become more resilient to changes in the economy, you are building a flow of business that carries you into the future. This may be true, but this also means that growth becomes a system 1 proposal, it is the most natural thought and your entire world is surrounding you with arguments that favour growth. But what if you make money in one segment and lose money in another; is growth still the best option? Maybe, but maybe not. The contrarian view would be to focus on the divestment of one segment and totally concentrate on the other, not to grow, but to shrink. This takes us back to what the purpose of the business is and what the stakeholders, and in particular the shareholders, have given management the mandate to do. Profit is the normal marching orders, but profit needs to be placed in relation to risk – a dynamic relationship. A decision, in line with shareholder requirements, may be to sell a part of the business, to pay out a cash dividend, and with a much smaller capital base operate a business with predictable and good margins. A higher return on capital and a strong future cash flow is the definition of value. Again, selling goes against the grain of system 1, which is why it may be so “attractive”.

Splitting the business

Most larger corporations have sub-businesses with different rationales, motivations and entirely different priorities. The challenge is that in most businesses there is an interconnecting relationship between departments and sub-businesses. The key question here is where top management should spend its time. A good exercise is to take the business through various potential combinations and study the potential value. It may be that a business should have separate management teams allowing a focus on different departments or organizational objectives.

In addition, and if a split is possible, maybe the businesses should not be part of the same legal unit. From a financial theory perspective, if parts of the business have different risk logic, it may be beneficial if they are not tied together. Similarly, the split units may be attractive to different investor segments. In the example opposite, we see how the blue corporation, a conglomerate, has a particular relationship with risk and return. Given the assumed risk level, one has a relatively low return on investment. By splitting the business into yellow and red companies, with each finding its interested investor segments, the returns on investment given their risks become higher.

The result is that the two companies have a higher value than the combined conglomerate. This is because these businesses are liked by their special segments while the conglomerate failed to attract a large investor following. Some may find it logical, but these are two entirely different risk and financing profiles and therefore they have fewer followers. Splitting the business into two units will immediately help in finding investor groups that may be willing to invest in the units that are more preferable for them. This, as a result, will increase the value of the organization on the whole.

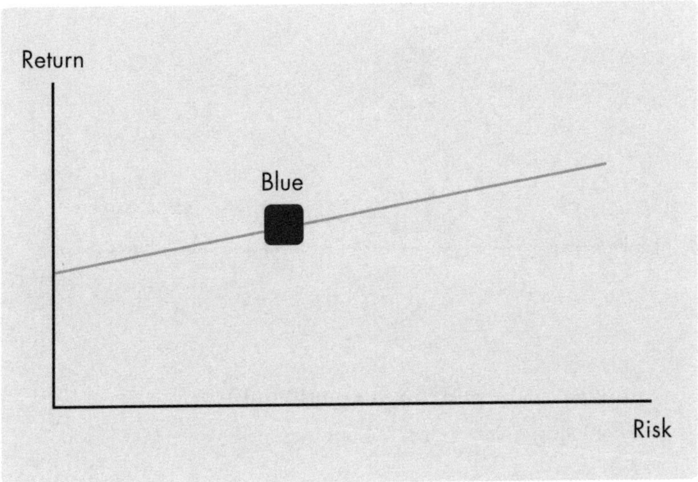

A typical conglomerate

Risk-Return profile of a typical conglommerate
with many sub-businesses.

The key question is whether the combination is attractive to the equity markets. Quite likely no, so split it. If parts of your business can be outsourced, you may reach the same contrarian view: sell it or give it away to someone that wants to run with it. See the graph below, where the initial risk/return profile is split to satisfy two different investor types:

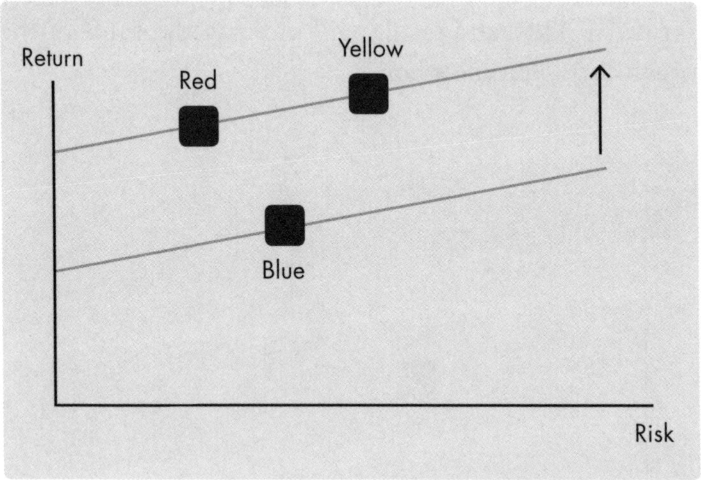

Splitting a conglomerate

By splitting a conglomerate into two parts, two Risk-Return profiles appealing to separate investor groups are created. The returns on investment given their risks become higher.

Merging with unequals

Rather than investing or raising capital from shareholders, investigate if it would be possible to merge with another company that has your customer base. This could also be a possibility when an organization does not have a great reputation, so they may be looking for alternative ways to boost value. A merger of interests could be where your company provides the business opportunity and your merger partner provides the listing with access to shareholders and capital markets.

Leveraging up

For many businesses that have a good position in a mature market, it may be difficult to select the right strategy going forward. It may be difficult and costly to increase the market share. An interesting perspective can be had from an outsourcing company in Sweden, where they leveraged up in order to secure value and to enhance management incentives. Rather than sell the company to outsiders, the owners started a new company and with the use of bank leverage, using the ongoing profitable activities as collateral, they sold the business to the new company. What did they achieve? Well, they were paid handsomely, they kept control of the business, and they managed to create new incentives for the management, to run fast and hard to be able to pay the interest and amortize down the new sizeable loans.

Changing crew

Business owners build loyalty to management but after a period of time the situation may become stale. The system 1 thought process that people possess gets them to build traditions and establish views on what is standard practice and how it should be done. By changing the members in each group, it may be possible to break traditions and create entirely new perspectives.

Is there risk in doing this? Sure, but possibly larger upsides by including people that see new things that the old were not able to see. Changing crew may also be the opportunity to lever up with new skills and knowledge, and take new perspectives on a stagnating business with tired ambitions.

Resilient means that you can survive difficult conditions, that you bounce back from adverse outcomes, that you are able to stand up to personal attacks and separate the people from the process. You should always try to see the best in the people and avoid mixing the relationship with the process or the decision at hand. If you do so, you will find it easier to deal with critique or the resistance that may build from you taking a different position than expected. This is directly connected to emotions – you may find it difficult to not be liked. But resilience also means survival, longevity and sustainability.

Inevitably, being contrarian and resilient is a long-term rather than a short-term action. By acting in this way, you are serving the purpose of the organization and its stakeholders, rather than acting in the interests of your fellow decision makers.

Resilience also means being able to recoil or spring back into shape after bending, stretching, or being compressed, so resilience is good, strong and useful in organizations. We can use golf to illustrate this point. A golf competition is usually played over four days and in the first days you see new names playing really well and the next day they are not even close to performing well. The people that end up winning, the valuable and purposeful players, play on the same level all four days and fight on in hard conditions, they play for the long-term, not the short-term. They have resilience.

How difficult is it to be resilient? It is tough. Our need to belong is one of our biggest strengths, but at the same time it is also one of our biggest weaknesses. Bearing this in mind, it is clear that it is easy to talk about being resilient, but this is completely different to actually being able to stand up when one is being disgraced by the surrounding tribe, be they right or wrong.

We are so included in social activities that it is almost difficult to comprehend what it is like to truly make up your own mind, to be able to think well and create value. The Indian philosopher Jiddu Krishnamurti said that "you need a mind that is capable of standing completely alone, not be burdened by the propaganda of others or the experiences of others. Enlightenment doesn't come through a leader, through a teacher, it comes through understanding of 'what is', which is in yourself, not running away from yourself. So, don't, if I may most respectfully suggest, join anything." Apply these strong words to your role as a decision maker and train your mind to resist the propaganda and body language of others when they are trying to convince you and have their way. You need to see that the arguments others communicate may not have anything to do with the issue at hand. Take a step back and analyze what is going on. Are others using theories and stories that are actually valid and do they truly understand them, or are they just communicating simplifications of the real situation you are reviewing? In the same way, what are the groups or tribes that the other people involved belong to that affect their considerations and proposed decisions? What is the agenda of others? Can you manage to shape a new agenda without being affected by the wishes or desires of others? It is true that the only way to truly add value is for you to find the answers within yourself, based on your own knowledge and experiences. So, the way to become a useful decision maker is to be strong and resilient and never back down to influences around you.

This book is about management decision making but for many people, business management and in particular finance is very abstract so it may be useful to make references to things that people feel more confident about, like art. Pablo Picasso is one of the most influential artists of the 20th century, one of the founders of the cubist movement and of the collage. One of his most famous works is Guernica, a dramatic painting of the bombing of the Spanish city by the German and Italian air-forces. It was typical Picasso to go through many phases of development and to make a radical change at the time he was becoming established in the genre. This ability to never become stale, always examining one's own position in search of something new, not allowing oneself to become dormant and stuck in system 1, seeing new solutions through conscious system 2 searches, is the mark of a contrarian. In fact, Picasso was so publicly opposed to older art that he was one of the people questioned by police when Mona Lisa was stolen in 1911. How would Picasso have been as a director or a top manager? Most likely he would not have been prejudiced and would have produced very unusual ideas when participating in business strategy sessions. Art is useful in understanding system 1 as it often throws us into new perspectives, out of system 1 and into system 2, by creating tension. What can we learn from Picasso? Firstly, to be a searcher, not resting on your laurels but progressing into new areas and, when successful, move again into the next area. Secondly, not being afraid of doing what had not been done before, resisting traditions; not letting established strategies control your potential. Thirdly, not letting anyone else capture your agenda, always maintaining control of purpose. Picasso could see that the established styles were nothing more than temporary, man-made constructs – the current myths.

12

Conclusion

This has been an introduction to some of the forces that affect human behaviour, or, in many cases, our lack of action. Initially, we went through system 1 and system 2, where I still see the main problem as being that people don't think that they have a problem and are content to stay in system 1. We are not aware of what is going on around us and we fail to analyze our way toward making good decisions. Lack of awareness is like a cognitive weakness that makes us behave poorly and make poor decisions. As a result, we risk making decisions that are not very ethical: our decisions are bad for most people around us because we don't use our brainpower. It is important to decide if we want to remain in system 1 and be followers or if we want to engage and get into system 2 more often. This is not applicable just to business; it is valid all over the place.

We also need to deal with traditions. We often hear people referring to a process as being a tradition, that it is sacred, and we should repeat what we have done previously. But traditions should be seen as an excellent opportunity to do something new and entirely different; they should be seen as an opportunity to create new traditions. If you want to be a contrarian, be sensitive to the use of traditions and analyze the potential outcome of doing something opposite to how things are normally done. Don't be afraid to change or break with old traditions to establish new ones.

We looked at the effects of tribalism, a powerful force that controls our behaviour in a sub-efficient way. You will see tribalism around you every day as we have a constant urge to belong, to be included, and this has a great effect on behaviour in organizations. The key is to ask yourself if the individual drive to belong is a good drive for making certain decisions. The answer is clear and by detecting new forms of tribalism you may find a better path to decision making.

We also discussed myths and the power included in paradigm myths, which cement the order we live by and coordinate our entire existence. It is important to see that they are man-made constructs and simplifications of complex relationships. We believe in myths and won't let them go until we find something better to believe in. This is why we hold on to the theories that generally don't work, but they are elegant and appear to be precise. They seem to be the solution to deepening our understanding while they are in fact decoys.

A problem with knowledge is that you can't just increase it by reading books about psychology or behavioural economics; you need to practice being a contrarian and gradually become more reflective, a person that can critically evaluate different, even contradictory paths. When you have practiced how to be a devil's advocate without creating difficult social situations, you are a resilient contrarian, a statesman. A challenge is also to be open to many difficult areas that make decision making more tedious. These may be powerful myths, powerful people trying to control our behaviour and, of course, the growing effects of modern tribalism. Study them, practice them, and you will be surprised over how present they are!

13

Selective Bibliography

Fama, Eugene and Stern, Joel. A look back at modern finance: Accomplishments and limitations. *Journal of applied corporate finance*, 28(4), 2016.

Harari, Yuval Noah. *Sapiens: a brief history of mankind*. Translated by the author, with the help of John Purcell and Haim Watzman. First published in Hebrew in Israel in 2011 by Kinneret, Zmora-Bitan, Dvir. Harper Perennial; Reprint edition May 15, 2018.

Kahneman, Daniel. *Thinking, Fast and Slow.* New York: Farrar, Straus and Giroux, 2011.

Lincoln, Bruce. *Discourse and the Construction of Society: Comparative Studies of Myth, Ritual, and Classification.* Oxford University Press, 2014.